VANISHINGS

Cover: A great carved head peers through the creeping Cambodian jungle, a sentinel of the once-magnificent temple complex of Angkor Wat and the long-vanished Khmer Empire.

VANISHINGS

By the Editors of Time-Life Books

TIME-LIFE BOOKS, ALEXANDRIA, VIRGINIA

CONTENTS

FATE UNKNOWN

The possibility of being made to vanish, to lose one's very self, taps such deep human fears that, in ages past, people blamed the devil or other dark forces for unexplained disappearances. Then as now, however, a vanishing is more likely to be an escape: Faced with overwhelming adversity, who would not dream of slipping anonymously into another life and place? In the United States alone, about one million people are added to the missing person rolls each year; almost all have merely dropped out of some frame of reference and reappear within six months.

Nonetheless, there remains a kind of aristocracy among the vanished, some real, some legendary, and all cloaked in the mythology of the inexplicably absent. Their disappearances often occur without visible motive, defy every rational explanation, and thwart even the most diligent investigator.

Lost at Z

One day in 1920, a British visitor to Brazil's national library in Rio de Janeiro came upon a yellowed parchment that riveted his attention. Prepared in the late eighteenth century, the manuscript described a hellish eleven-year odyssey through the dense jungle of the Mato Grosso—and a remarkable discovery.

On a quartz-face cliff in the forest, the Portuguese explorers had discovered an ancient staircase cut into the rock, leading to a massive stone portal. Beyond this entrance they saw a lost city of wide avenues, statuary, temples, and other buildings, all constructed in a style like that of ancient Greece. The surrounding marshes and fallow fields were rich with game. Inscriptions in an unknown language—copied in the document—adorned the gateway.

For Colonel Percy Harrison Fawcett, the story had the ring of truth. A military engineer by trade, the fifty-three-year-old Briton had sought lost cities in the jungles of Ceylon as well as South America. Only a few years before, he had completed an arduous three-year survey of what he called "a long and excessively unhealthy sector of the Brazilian-Bolivian frontier," establishing the first real boundary in the contested area. His work had an almost mystical dimension. "The forest in these solitudes," he wrote, "is always full of voices, soft whisperings." But the ruin evoked by the old parchment was more than a whisper. Fawcett believed he knew the location of this legendary city—Z, as he called it—from other sources he did not disclose.

Later that same year, he set out

Camp (his horse had died there in 1920), brought back by the two guides, who were afraid to go farther into hostile territory. "You need have no fear of failure," Fawcett wrote. Then, silence.

Because his family understood the difficulty of communicating from the interior jungles, the first search party was not sent out until 1928. They found a small trunk believed to be Fawcett's and were told that hostile natives had killed the three white men soon after they entered the heavy forest. But Indians drove the rescuers out of the region before they could confirm the stories. Fawcett remained a mystery—and a dangerous magnet for all who followed. In 1930, American reporter Albert de Winton tried to track Fawcett down, but he, too, vanished in the jungle without a trace. A year later, a Swiss trapper named Stefan Rattin reported that he had come upon an old Englishman living as a well-cared-for prisoner among a group of Indians. Although the man had not given his name, Rattin's de-

scription and the man's circumstances raised hopes that Fawcett had at last been found. But when Rattin returned to rescue the putative Fawcett, he and two partners also disappeared.

For decades afterward, Mato Grosso travelers reported meeting gaunt, English-speaking oldsters along jungle paths. But no real trace of the British explorer or his two companions was ever found. There have been reports of blue-eyed, white-skinned Indians in the rain forest, said to be offspring of young Jack Fawcett. Bones unearthed in 1950 and identified as Fawcett's did not, in fact, match the descriptions of any of the three explorers. And there has been speculation that Fawcett's supposed route of march was entirely fictitious—that he had taken quite another path to Z and vanished. In the view of some Brazilian cults that sprang up around the mystery of his disappearance, the redoubtable explorer survived the gauntlet of hostile tribes and lives on in the lost city only he could find. □

on his first quest. This expedition was cut short by his companions, who quickly had their fill of aggressive insects, deadly snakes, blood-sucking bats, exotic diseases, and tangled undergrowth.

In 1925, now fifty-eight, Fawcett tried again, this time financed by newspaper companies hungry for his story and by England's Royal Geographical Society. On April 20, he marched out of the Brazilian frontier town of Cuyabá, taking as companions only his son Jack, his son's eighteen-year-old friend Raleigh Rimell, and two Mufuquas Indians, and following a secret route he had shared with no one.

In November, a message written on May 30 arrived in Rio from a point Fawcett called Dead Horse

Emissary to Oblivion

About midday on November 25, 1809, a four-horse post chaise clattered into the courtyard of an inn at Perleberg, a few miles east of the river Elbe on the Berlin-Hamburg road. A tall man stepped out, elegantly clad in a fine, velvet-lined sable coat, a matching fur hat, well-tailored gray trousers, and a cravat set off by a large diamond. He called himself Baron von Koch, a traveling merchant; but it

was clear to all concerned that he was not what he purported to be.

In fact, he was twenty-five-year-old Benjamin Bathurst, on his way back to England after a precocious diplomatic coup in Austria. He had been sent to the Vienna court of Emperor Francis earlier in the year by his powerful kinsman Earl Bathurst. The young diplomat's secret mission was to persuade Francis, who had just raised a ◊

Colonel Percy Harrison Fawcett is shown before a backdrop of the deadly Brazilian jungle, where he would later disappear in 1925 in search of the legendary city that he called Z.

300,000-man militia, to attack France. The British, then planning a major assault on Napoleon's forces in the west, wanted France's attention diverted eastward. The emissary had succeeded brilliantly, although the Austrian troops met a humiliating defeat and signed a disadvantageous peace accord with France in October.

Whatever the outcome for his hosts, Bathurst's mission had ended, and he set out for England. Worried that the French emperor had marked him for assassination, he chose a roundabout itinerary via Berlin and Sweden, and traveled with a servant, a secretary, and a pair of loaded pistols. At Perleberg, however, his route passed perilously close to the French forces pulled up across the Elbe.

Suddenly nervous, Bathurst requested military protection from the town's garrison commander, a Captain Klitzing, explaining that something disturbing had happened to him since his arrival; he did not elaborate. With two soldiers to guard him, he returned to the post house and spent the early evening writing letters—and burning some documents. At 7 p.m., he dismissed the soldiers and ordered his carriage for 9 o'clock. Shortly before his scheduled departure, Bathurst went out to check on his horses. Eyewitnesses said later that they had seen him standing by the heads of the team, his features dimly illuminated by lantern light. The next moment he was gone. An intensive, town-wide search failed to turn up the missing diplomat, but his fur coat was discovered hidden in a nearby basement. Three weeks later, a peasant woman found Bathurst's bullet-torn, but strangely blood-

less, trousers in a nearby woods. A pocket held an unfinished letter to Bathurst's wife, Phillida, expressing his fear of a certain Count D'Entraigues and begging Phillida not to remarry should something befall her spouse.

Phillida and Benjamin's sister, a Mrs. Thistlethwayte, both traveled to the Continent to conduct investigations of their own, clinging to the belief that Bathurst had been abducted by the French. In fact, the sinister count mentioned in Bathurst's last letter eventually contacted Mrs. Bathurst and reported that her husband had been swept up in a French search for spies. The agents had incarcerated Bathurst, he said, in the nearby fortress of Magdeburg and executed him before they realized who he was. D'Entraigues—by reputation a double spy for Russia and France—vowed to provide proof from Paris. But, in what appears to have been an unrelated calamity, he and his wife were murdered by a servant before he could do so. Captain Klitzing, however, blamed not the French but the motley crew assembled around the post house in Perleberg. After one of these suspects died, a skeleton some thought was Bathurst's was discovered under the stone flooring of his house.

Another possibility is that Bathurst's fears of a vengeful Napoleon were well grounded—that the French leader, furious at Bathurst's role in sending Austria against him, had arranged the young man's murder. If that was the case, it carried a splendid irony. The man who sent Bonaparte to his final exile on St. Helena in 1815 was the British Secretary of State for War and the Colonial Department—Earl Bathurst. □

Arctic Vise

In the mid-nineteenth century, the British Admiralty became captivated by the arctic waters north of Canada. Fearful of Russian expansionism in the area, the Royal Navy hoped to find a direct route from the Atlantic to the Pacific—the so-called Northwest Passage. Part of it had been charted. But no mariner had penetrated the waters that threaded around Prince of Wales, Victoria, and King William islands, then turned westward toward the Beaufort Sea. The conditions there were surpassingly grim: harsh winds, barren land, and waterways choked with ice.

In 1844, the Admiralty began looking for someone fit to command an expedition into the uncharted reaches of the Northwest Passage. Among the candidates was Sir John Franklin, a bluff, tenacious, and experienced officer and arctic hand, who had returned

HMS *Erebus* is caught in arctic ice in this depiction of the ill-fated search for the Northwest Passage by John Franklin *(left)*. His second-in-command, Francis Crozier *(right)*, sent the stranded crew on a fatal march toward land.

from a stint as governor of Tasmania. At fifty-nine, Franklin was old for the job but desperately eager. Warned a retired arctic explorer, "If you don't let him go, the man will die of disappointment." Franklin won the assignment.

Franklin set out on May 19, 1845, with some 130 men aboard the 340-ton former gunship *Terror* and her 370-ton sister *Erebus*, provisioned for three years. In Baffin Bay two weeks later, Sir John and his officers dined with a Scottish whaling captain—the last European to see the explorers alive. After the Franklin party failed to return as planned, rescue parties were dispatched, and near the end of 1850, one of them found traces of one of the explorers' first camps. More than three years later, Hudson's Bay Company employee John Rae, traveling overland, met a band of Eskimos who carried

knives and forks from the Franklin Expedition and told of seeing white men's bodies ravaged by cannibalism. The British government paid Rae the proffered £10,000 reward and tried to close the case.

But Lady Jane Franklin would not give up hope of learning her husband's fate. She helped to outfit a yacht called the *Fox*, under the command of Francis McClintock, to continue the search. On July 1, 1857, McClintock sailed for Canada and twenty months later had dispatched sled expeditions to search King William Island. One of his men found a pile of rocks containing two messages by Lieutenant Graham Gore of the *Erebus*. The first, dated May 28, 1847, reported that all was well. The other, dated April 25, 1848, described how the desperate expedition came to the end of its tether.

Apparently, Franklin's party

spent the first winter on a rocky outcropping known as Beechey Island, due north of the area they intended to explore. Three of his men died and were buried there. In the next fleeting arctic summer, Franklin sailed south. He groped his way through the lane known as Peel Sound and eventually reached King William Island, just off the mainland. And there he made a fatal mistake.

Based on information from a previous expedition, his maps showed King William as a peninsula, not an island. As a result, Franklin steered a course that took him into an area of water known as the Victoria Strait, which is choked with ice year-round. The floes trapped, then inexorably tightened their grip on, the two vessels. By September 12, 1846, the ships were held in a frozen vise. They spent the winter locked in place. ◊

His face frozen in an eternal grimace, petty officer John Torrington of the HMS *Terror* stares up from his coffin on Beechey Island, where he was exhumed by anthropologists in 1984.

Franklin died in June 1847 of an unrecorded cause. Under his second-in-command, Captain Francis Crozier, the ships continued their southward drift in the ice and into another dreadful winter that claimed 23 more lives. With scurvy spreading through the crew, Crozier decided on a desperate gamble. He ordered his remaining men to start a frigid march across King William Island toward the mainland, in the hope of reaching an outlying post of the Hudson Bay Trading Company. Diseased and starving, the men set forth in April 1848. The strongest made it across the ice to the mainland, but no farther. No one survived. The vanished expedition has remained a kind of magnet for other arctic hands. In the 1870s, American Army lieutenant Frederick Schwatka discovered the bones of the last survivors on the mainland. And a century later, in 1984, a Canadian anthropology team exhumed the bodies that Franklin had buried on Beechey Island in 1846. Examination of the remains—remarkably well preserved in the arctic chill—revealed that ice had not been Franklin's only enemy: Lead poisoning, from the inferior soldering of food tins, may have further weakened the doomed explorers. □

Outback Eccentric

When Ludwig Leichhardt arrived in 1842, Australia had been thoroughly explored only along its southern fringes. There were no great river systems, as in North and South America, to lead explorers into the dry, harsh interior.

Few men were less prepared than Leichhardt to reconnoiter this wilderness. The dreamy son of a Prussian farmer, he had studied at the universities of Göttingen and Berlin, aiming to be a doctor. There is no record that he succeeded. In October 1840, he deserted from the army and fled to Sydney.

Leichhardt was known for his eccentric ways. He wore a Chinese coolie hat and carried a sword, because he was said to be terrified of firearms. His eyesight was as bad as his sense of direction. Nevertheless, he yearned to be the first to explore the land route from south to north along Australia's Great Dividing Range from Sydney to Port Essington, a settlement near the continent's northern tip.

He assembled a rag-tag crew and convinced well-to-do Australians to finance the trek. Ill-equipped, his troop of eight set off from the fertile region known as the Darling Downs in September 1844. Never straying more than ten miles from running water (they had not brought enough canteens), the group reached the eastern edge of the Gulf of Carpentaria in June 1845. There, naturalist John Gilbert was killed in an Aboriginal attack, and two other men were wounded. The surviving band traveled along the edge of the gulf and six months later stumbled into Port Essington. They returned by sea to Sydney, where they had been given up for dead.

The expedition made Leichhardt the most famous man in Australia. Citizens took up collections for him, and foreign geographical societies bestowed medals. The king of Prussia pardoned him for desertion. All of that stimulated Leichhardt to plan an even more spectacular journey.

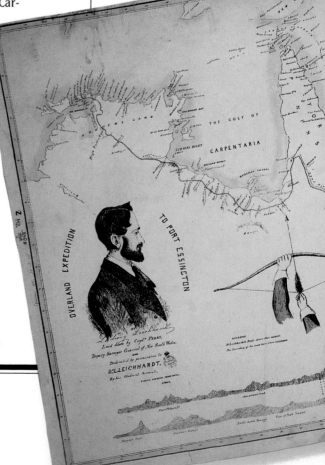

This time he would start once more from the Darling Downs, head north again for Carpentaria, then strike west all the way across the continent. His route would take him through hostile tribal lands and across some of the world's most forbidding deserts. Once again, he recruited a group of eight followers and convinced backers to provide him with supplies. Carrying two years' supplies and accompanied by a herd of sheep, goats, and cattle, he set out in December 1846, the hottest time of year. Eight months later, he was back. His party had wandered aimlessly and lost their livestock. According to one account, Leichhardt had given strange commands, telling his followers, for example, to cook game with the entrails left in, which led to bouts of sickness. When his own supplies ran low, he filched from others. Eventually, they gave up in disgust and despair. Despite this fiasco, Leich-hardt was able to find backers for another expedition. In April 1848, he set forth with six mates, fifty head of cattle, twenty mules, and seven horses. Somewhere on their journey, the entire party, man and beast, disappeared without a trace.

Rumors about Leichhardt's fate continued to crop up for years. It was said that he had been killed by Aborigines or drowned in flash floods. There were tales of a wild white man in the bush, living with natives, possibly a survivor of the lost expedition. At least two of Leichhardt's camps were discovered, and at various places in the interior, trees were found marked with a mysterious *L*. In 1880, the Sydney *Bulletin* coined the term *Franklin of Australian exploration*, ranking Leichhardt's final foray with Sir John Franklin's ill-fated arctic probe *(page 10)*.

Leichhardt himself had long since been embedded in official Australian lore. Plaques marked various sites along his first expeditionary trail. In the state of Queensland, where most of his early exploring took place, a mountain range and a river were named after him. In Sydney, a suburb earned the same distinction, and his surname identifies twenty varieties of Australian plants.

In 1938, an expedition headed by the president of the Royal Geographic Society of South Australia went to the edge of the Simpson Desert, deep in the center of the country, drawn by rumors that seven or eight skeletons were lying there. The party found only unidentifiable fragments of bone and teeth, and two coins—a half-sovereign and a Maundy three-pence, both minted before the doomed expedition left Sydney. □

The Lady Disappears

Not long before the opening of the French capital's Great Exposition of 1889, a distraught young Englishwoman rushed into the British embassy in Paris and told a story that has reverberated through fantasy and fiction ever since. She and her mother were on their way home from India and, owing to the shortage of accommodations in the crowded city, had taken two single rooms in a hotel. The mother chose room 342, decorated with rose-strewn wallpaper and plum-colored velvet curtains. Then the older woman collapsed on the bed.

After examining the prostrate guest and talking excitedly in French with the hotel manager, the house doctor told the young woman that her mother was seriously ill and must have some medicine. But the proper medication could be found only in his office on the other side of town. The daughter would have to take his carriage and carry a note to his wife, who would hand her the drugs.

What should have been a simple errand consumed four hours. The driver kept the horses to an amble and seemed to steer in circles, and the doctor's wife took a long time to produce the medicine.

Finally, the frustrated daughter arrived back at the hotel, only to discover that all queries about her mother were met with blank stares. "I know nothing of your mother," said the manager. "You arrived here alone." The doctor was similarly confused by the woman's questions. Frantic now, the young traveler examined the hotel register. Instead of her mother's ◊

A nineteenth-century commemorative map celebrates the eccentric Ludwig Leichhardt's arduous fifteen-month trek from Sydney to Port Essington, Australia, along the previously unexplored Great Dividing Range.

familiar signature, she saw a stranger's beside room 342. Insisting on looking at the room itself, she found no velvet curtains, no flowered wallpaper, no familiar baggage—only the luggage of strangers. At this point, she fled to the embassy, where she was received with sympathy—and general disbelief. Trapped in a nightmare, the young woman ended her days in a British mental hospital.

This chilling tale has inspired at least two novels and a film—Alfred Hitchcock's *The Lady Vanishes.* But no one has been able to verify that it ever happened, and no supporting documents have been unearthed at the British Foreign Office or elsewhere. Even the *Detroit Free Press* journalist who first reported this vanishing story could not remember whether he had covered or created it. □

Three Against the Sea

From the time of its completion in December 1899 on Eilean Mor, a rocky island some eighty miles west of the Scottish coast, the lighthouse seemed cursed. In its first year of operation, three keepers died, a fourth fell to his death from the lantern gallery, and several went mad. Then, on December 15, 1900, the light went out.

The lighthouse was operated by a crew of four, with three men on duty and one ashore. On December 20, Joseph Moore, the off-duty lighthouse keeper, was due to return to Eilean Mor from the nearby Hebrides to relieve one of his three colleagues, but bad weather prevented his arrival until December 26. As the supply boat approached the lighthouse, the place was eerily calm. No keepers came to greet the boat, no flag was flying, and the empty provision boxes had not been set out on the landing. Moore went ashore and mounted the steep stairs cut into the cliff on which the lighthouse stood.

He found everything in order in the lightroom except one feature: The light's lens had been cleaned but not covered. Since the keepers would normally cover the lens soon after cleaning it, it appeared that someone had been interrupted at his work. An untouched meal of meat, pickles, and potatoes waited on the table, and one of the dining chairs was overturned. Two oilskin coats were missing.

The island's west landing showed signs of a violent storm earlier in December. A wooden box containing ropes had been torn from its place 110 feet above sea level. Gigantic waves had twisted the iron railings on the landing and torn away turf from the cliff top itself, 200 feet above high tide. But on the drizzly day of the keepers' disappearance, the tempest had passed. "Storm ended," read the December 15 weather log, "Sea calm. God is over all." All, it seemed, but the three hapless lighthouse keepers.

Their disappearance was attributed variously to abduction by a sea monster, kidnapping by foreign agents, snatching by a giant seabird, and the angry intervention of a ghost said to police the island against intruders. Some believed that one of the keepers had killed his comrades before taking his own life. But the official investigation concluded that the three men must have been washed away when a monstrous wave surprised them on the landing. □

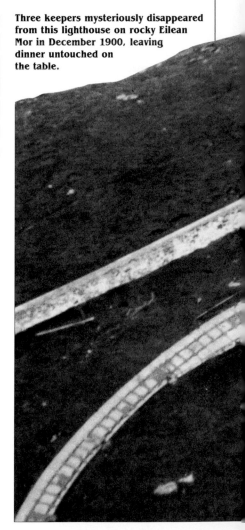

Three keepers mysteriously disappeared from this lighthouse on rocky Eilean Mor in December 1900, leaving dinner untouched on the table.

A Baffling Brig

In the annals of disappearance at sea, one name is intriguing and evocative beyond all the rest: *Mary Celeste*. More than 115 years after the fact—and after innumerable fictional treatments and speculative articles—authorities cannot explain the most famous nautical vanishing of the modern age.

The puzzle began to unfold on December 5, 1872, when the British cargo vessel *Dei Gratia* sighted a brig, with two sails blown away, wallowing in the North Atlantic midway between the Azores and Portugal. For Captain David Moorehouse of the *Dei Gratia*, the strange ship's name was a nasty surprise. He had dined aboard the 103-foot, 282-ton *Mary Celeste*

with her captain, Benjamin Spooner Briggs, on November 3, as the two vessels loaded cargo side-by-side in New York City's East River. Days later, the *Mary Celeste* had set sail for Genoa bearing 1,700 barrels of raw alcohol. With Briggs and his crew of seven were the captain's wife, Sarah, and their two-year-old daughter, Sophia.

A three-man boarding party found the larder well stocked but no one aboard the stricken ship. A lifeboat was missing, and in the main cabin, a woman's clothes and a child's toys were scattered about. The seamen's belongings remained in the crew's quarters. In the mate's cabin, a slate bore the scrawled start of a letter to "Fanny, my dear wife." The ship's compass and navigational instruments were broken or missing. The last entry in the ship's log was dated November 25: Evidently, the *Mary Celeste* had sailed unguided for more than a week and had covered 700 miles.

The ship appeared to be only slightly damaged. Two of the cargo

hatches had blown open, and about three feet of seawater had washed into the hold. A barrel of the alcohol cargo had been staved in, and there was a gash on one rail, identified as an ax cut. The only sign of possible foul play was a stained sword discovered beneath one of the bunks.

Yet when Moorehouse brought the *Mary Celeste* to Gibraltar, the issue of foul play was immediately raised by British officials at an inquiry. In the investigators' opinion, the gash, the sword, and the spilled alcohol all pointed to a drunken mutiny in which the crew killed the captain and his family, then escaped by lifeboat. The vessel's American owners, however, pointed out that the skipper was well liked by his men and ran a nondrinking ship. Besides, the kind of alcohol that was on board the *Mary Celeste* would cause severe stomach pain and eventual blindness if consumed. And if they had indeed mutinied, why had the sailors left their sea chests behind?

Eventually, the inquiry ruled that

No sign of Captain Benjamin Briggs (*left*), his family, or his crew was found aboard the *Mary Celeste* (*above*) on December 5, 1872, when the *Dei Gratia* discovered the abandoned two-masted vessel adrift in the North Atlantic.

the *Mary Celeste* mystery was unsolved. The *Dei Gratia* was awarded salvage fees, and the *Mary Celeste's* owners soon sold her.

In 1882, a young British writer-physician named Arthur Conan Doyle wrote a story about the disappearance of everyone aboard a ship named the *Marie Celeste.* Doyle's fictional account caused a sensation and greatly boosted the career of the man who would later create Sherlock Holmes. It also prompted new theories about the fate of the mystery ship's vanished crew. One explanation had it that the unlucky group was taken by Barbary pirates—even though that menace had been eradicated long before the *Mary Celeste* set sail. A competing notion was that a giant squid had devoured everyone on board, while yet another theory guessed that the crew had eaten food contaminated with the ergot fungus, found on tainted rye bread, which can cause convulsions and insanity. The deranged crew then fled, only to die at sea.

Perhaps the most compelling scenario revolves around some trouble with the volatile cargo of alcohol, as suggested by the cracked barrel and burst hatches. Wanting to get off the ship as explosions threatened, but unwilling at this point to abandon his vessel, Captain Briggs would have ordered his family and crew members into lifeboats, which could be safely towed behind the *Mary Celeste* until the danger had passed. The line linking the lifeboats to their mother ship had accidentally parted, however, leaving them drifting in the wake of the *Mary Celeste* as she sailed into legend. □

Good-bye, Dolly

Plump, pretty, twenty-five-year-old Dorothy Arnold—niece of a U.S. Supreme Court justice, daughter of a successful businessman, descendant of a passenger on the *Mayflower*—had returned from Bryn Mawr to live under her parents' sumptuous Manhattan roof. On December 12, 1910, she stepped out to shop and, in the early afternoon, chatted on the sidewalk with a friend. Then, as one contemporary journalist described it, Dorothy Arnold "disappeared from one of the busiest streets on earth, at the sunniest hour of a brilliant ◊

afternoon, with thousands within sight and reach, men and women who knew her on every side, and officers of the law thickly strewn about her path."

When their daughter failed to return, the Arnolds first contacted her friends, then a series of detectives. Not until six weeks later did the Arnolds speak to the police, who urged the staid seventy-three-year-old father, Francis Arnold, to use the press to publicize the disappearance. Meeting with reporters, Francis Arnold declared that his daughter must have been murdered in Central Park and thrown into the lake or the reservoir. The interview also gave skeptical newsmen a chance to query Arnold about Dorothy's love life. He exploded, ranting against "men who have nothing to do."

That, journalists soon discovered, aptly described pudgy, forty-two-year-old George Griscom, Jr., who lived with his parents and called himself Junior. Under the guise of visiting a former college classmate, Dorothy had spent a week with Junior, unchaperoned, in Boston—a scandal in 1910.

Nor was Junior Griscom the only wild card in Dorothy's life. She had begun writing short stories and asked her parents to let her move to an apartment in Greenwich Village to continue her work. A furious father had thundered, "Good writers can write anywhere!"—and that had been that. When Dorothy's first short story was rejected by a magazine, her family teased her mercilessly about her literary pretentions. After a second short story was rejected, Dorothy wrote to

Junior, then vacationing with his parents in Italy, that the magazine "has turned me down. Failure stares me in the face. All I can see ahead is a long road with no turning." Then, ominously: "Mother will always think an accident has happened." A few weeks later, Dorothy Arnold was gone.

Cabled in Florence, Griscom sent back the message "Know absolutely nothing." And, on a surprise visit in Italy from Dorothy's brother and mother, Junior apparently had nothing more to offer than a packet of Dorothy's letters.

In 1921, the head of the New York City Department of Missing Persons told a high school assembly that Dorothy Arnold's fate had always been known to her family and the police. Questioned later, he recanted, insisting he had been misquoted. In 1935, twenty-five years after Arnold vanished, people were still calling the police to report sightings of the heiress.

Many theories were advanced to explain the young woman's disappearance. Some said that she must have killed herself, perhaps inspired by Junior's cousin, who had committed suicide when he was not permitted to marry an English governess. One theory held that she had been whisked away to Mexico by white slavers, another that she had died under the knife of a back-alley abortionist, and yet another that she was alive and happy in Honolulu. A supernaturalist noted that the day after her disappearance, a lovely white swan appeared in Central Park. Obviously, he said, the restless girl had been transmuted into a bird. □

An Ancient Mariner

Born on a farm among the ship-building centers of Nova Scotia in 1844, Joshua Slocum longed to sail the tall ships that pervaded his childhood. He went to sea at age sixteen and was captain of a sailing ship when only twenty-five. But he was a man out of his time: The skipper who would become known as the world's best sailor lived in a world that had changed to steam.

Straining against the tide of new technology, Slocum eked out an increasingly meager living from his sail-driven ships. Always accompanied by Virginia, his Australian wife, he hauled cargo and fish, and tried to keep his rowdy crews in line. Virginia bore seven children and schooled them in all the basics, including music, for which a piano had been bolted to the deck. But the hard life at sea proved more than she could bear: She died in 1884, at thirty-four. After her death, one of their sons recalled much later, "Father never recovered. He was like a ship with a broken rudder."

The changing world of sea transport only made matters worse for Joshua Slocum, as steam-driven competitors reduced the work of sailing vessels to odd jobs. In 1892, on the beach and shipless, Slocum had a critical windfall. A retired whaling captain offered to give him an ancient oysterman, which Slocum happily accepted and began to refurbish. After thirteen months' hard labor on this new vessel, the *Spray*, as he proudly wrote of her, "sat on the water like a swan."

While renovating the *Spray*,

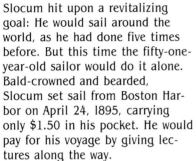

Slocum hit upon a revitalizing goal: He would sail around the world, as he had done five times before. But this time the fifty-one-year-old sailor would do it alone. Bald-crowned and bearded, Slocum set sail from Boston Harbor on April 24, 1895, carrying only $1.50 in his pocket. He would pay for his voyage by giving lectures along the way.

More than three years and 46,000 miles of ocean after his departure, Slocum returned home, the first man to circumnavigate the globe on a solo voyage. Upon converting his experience into the book *Sailing Alone around the World,* Slocum earned global renown and became the honored guest of President Theodore Roosevelt and wealthy yachtsmen.

But Slocum's life soon began to drift again. An effort to live ◊

Sailing alone on his beloved old oyster-man, the *Spray*—shown above in Australian waters—Joshua Slocum circumnavigated the globe at the turn of the century. In 1909, he set out on a final voyage, possibly to find the source of the Amazon, and never returned.

ashore as a Martha's Vineyard farmer with his second wife, Hettie, ended with his return to the *Spray*. Aboard the boat he loved, Slocum wandered along American rivers and coastlines, with winter forays into the warm Caribbean waters. Living on the *Spray* in the early years of this century, and, as he wrote Victor, his eldest son, "hustling for a dollar," Slocum imagined another dramatic voyage: a solo journey to the then-unknown source of the Amazon River. On November 14, 1909, the *Spray* glided out of Martha's Vineyard, southbound. No one knows whether Slocum was on his way to the Amazon or to another winter in the Cayman Islands: The *Spray* and her

captain vanished soon after sailing from Martha's Vineyard. A few mariners believe Slocum and his vessel finally met a storm capable of sinking them, but that is a minority view; they had ridden out some of the world's worst weather. Others see the disappearance as Slocum's way of ending a life that had become increasingly meaningless to him. But in a 1950 biography of his father, Victor Slocum proposed that the end must have come from the great machines that had displaced the sail. Crossing busy Atlantic shipping lanes, he speculated, the poorly lighted *Spray* had been run down in the night by a passing steamer.

A story from the Antilles that

began circulating in the 1950s seems evidence for such a fate, although it puts Slocum farther south than anyone had dreamed. According to a Turtle Island planter, Slocum stayed with him for a few days late in 1909, then headed south. Two days later, the planter saw an incoming 500-ton steamer with a gash on her hull just above the waterline—the result, the captain said, of running down a native boat the night before. But the second mate, on whose watch the accident occurred, said there had been no one at the helm of the sunken boat, which "was not a native of this area." The planter concluded that the hapless vessel must have been the *Spray*. □

The Natural

A rising young star of Edwardian politics, Albert Victor Grayson was called "the greatest mob orator of all time." Some said that he might have become Britain's prime minister. But he is remembered best today as the center of a deep political mystery, for in September 1920, the thirty-nine-year-old Socialist stepped into the night and was never seen again.

Seventh son of a poor Liverpool carpenter, Grayson discovered his gift for oratory at a tender age. While attending Manchester's Home Missionary College, he became a well-known radical voice at street-corner assemblies. Soon he left school to pursue a career in politics and journalism.

In a stunning 1907 upset, Grayson, then only twenty-five, was elected to the House of Commons

as a Socialist. Once seated, the young gadfly ignored Parliament's time-honored traditions and used the House as a platform for his sometimes strident views. Grayson's arrogance and independence annoyed more conservative members, leading at one point to his suspension. Partly because of allegations that he enjoyed the high life, Grayson's pro-temperance constituents failed to reelect him in 1910. Although he took this defeat in stride, his fortunes never quite recovered.

In 1912, Grayson married Ruth Nightingale, a tempestuous Shakespearean actress, with whom he traveled widely—to America in 1913 and then on tour in Australia and New Zealand from 1915 to 1917.

A staunch advocate of the war against Germany, Grayson enlisted in the New Zealand Expeditionary Force and served until wounded. By then a heavy drinker, Grayson faced bankruptcy court soon after peace returned. In 1918, his adored wife and her second baby died in childbirth. A distraught Grayson sent his only child, Elaine, to live with Ruth's parents. A year later, he told a friend he was in desperate straits, adding, "I'll be glad to get out of it all."

But Grayson had one final cause: to expose the trade in peerages and titles. He labeled the selling of these honors a national scandal and swore to reveal the culpable "monocled dandy with offices in Whitehall"—a thoroughfare often used as a synonym for the British government. His attacks earned him the enmity of a sinister figure Grayson knew from his wife's acting days: Maundy Gregory, a former theater manager who ran the honors sales for his political boss, Prime Minister David Lloyd George.

A year later, in 1920, Grayson vanished. Some stories say he left his mother's house in Liverpool en route to a speaking engagement, rounded a corner, and disappeared. Other reports have Grayson last seen in a London hotel bar, where after receiving a note, he excused himself, said he would return shortly, and walked out, leaving behind his coat and suitcase.

Explanations advanced for his disappearance included sudden amnesia, suicide, and a secret marriage to a rich widow. Some believe he was silenced with money or murder by Maundy Gregory. But most students of the case believe he merely opted for a new life with a new identity. Credible reports of seeing Grayson in England came in 1924, 1928, and 1932. In 1939, a close friend asserted that he had seen Grayson with a woman, both prosperously dressed, on the London underground. The woman called her companion "Vic," and when the two exited near Parliament, both of them laughed as the man said, "Here's the old firm." By the time the onlooker realized why "Vic" looked familiar, it was too late to catch him.

Mysterious as it is, Grayson's fate may be no less puzzling than his origins. One of the remarkable aspects of the young orator was the gentlemanly ease with which he met the world, his naturally aristocratic poise and appearance, and the apparent liquidity of his "poor" family. According to one recent biographer, Grayson may have inherited his uppercrust traits not from the Liverpudlian who gave him his name, but from a real father who paid the Graysons to raise an illegitimate son.

When Ruth Nightingale's mother lay dying, she is said to have taken her granddaughter's hand and repeated "the Marlboroughs" over and over. A trusted servant told Elaine Grayson, "Your grandmother was telling you who your father really was"—a secret descendant of the duke of Marlborough, whose surname was Churchill. □

The charismatic Albert Victor Grayson harangues English voters in 1906. In the following year, the young Socialist was swept into the House of Commons in a stunning upset victory.

Farmers' Tales

As the story has it, David Lang, a Tennessee farmer, stepped off his porch the afternoon of September 23, 1880, strode across a field, and as his astonished wife and children and two other witnesses looked on, vanished into thin air.

Just as perplexing was the 1889 case of eleven-year-old Oliver Larch of South Bend, Indiana, who vanished on his way to a well on Christmas Eve. Moments after the boy set out, the assembled guests heard Oliver yell for help. But they found only his footprints in the newly fallen snow—the trail began at the door and abruptly ended only halfway to the well.

These stories are two of the better known examples of a certain species of vanishing tale that is rendered real by names, dates, locations, and rich detail but ultimately elusive. Since the anecdotes are so poignant and exert such power on the imagination, intrigued researchers have attempted to verify them.

A study of local records revealed no mention of a David Lang in Sumner County, where he was supposed to have farmed. But it did turn up the name of renowned local citizen Joe Mulhatten, a notable teller of tall tales who reportedly won a lying contest with the help of imaginary farmer Lang. Oliver Larch turned out to be no more real than David Lang. Larch does not appear in county records, police documents, census reports, or newspapers of the time; and weather records show there was no snow to accept his footprints on that Christmas Eve.

Nevertheless, these stories continue to circulate, some changing to fit the times. For instance, the Lang disappearance, once attributed to fairies, was seen by some in the 1970s as the work of extraterrestrials. □

Old Gringo

Born in 1842 on an Ohio farm, Ambrose Gwinnett Bierce was the tenth of thirteen children. He left home at fifteen and, three years later, joined the Union Army. Rising from drummer boy to first lieutenant, he saw action at Shiloh, Chickamauga, Murfreesboro, Franklin, and Nashville. According to his brother Albert, a severe head wound received near Atlanta made Bierce "bitter and suspicious."

After the Civil War, Bierce tried a succession of jobs before turning to journalism in San Francisco. His cynicism and caustic wit, liberally applied to the public figures of the day, earned him the epithet Wickedest Man in San Francisco. His darkly humorous stories led admirers to rank him with Edgar Allan Poe, and he soon became the most renowned writer west of the Rocky Mountains. His initials, A. G., according to one writer, stood for Almighty God. Despite a jaundiced view of matrimony, the dashing cynic married in 1871 and, a year later, moved to London. There he met Mark Twain, continued his journalism, and published his first three books. Their contents reflect Bierce's typically macabre preoccupations: In one, a child is eaten by a dog. London friends nicknamed the writer Bitter Bierce.

Back in San Francisco in 1875, Bierce returned to journalism and eventually joined young William Randolph Hearst at the *San Francisco Examiner.* But Bierce's life was becoming as grim as his outlook. In 1889, his elder son killed a rival, then himself. Bierce's only other son died of pneumonia in 1901 after a prodigious binge. Mollie, Bierce's hapless wife, died

just before their divorce decree became final, of what was called heart failure.

In 1909, aged sixty-seven and working in Washington, D.C., Bierce left the Hearst organization to assemble his twelve-volume collected works, and then, it appears, began to hint at the dramatic twist his own life might take. "If you hear of my being stood up against a Mexican stone wall and shot to rags, please know that I think that a pretty good way to depart this life," the old curmudgeon wrote a nephew's wife. "To be Gringo in Mexico, ah, that is euthanasia!"

He headed south early in 1913, stopping to visit some of the Civil War battlefields where he had fought as a young man and where he appears to have been most fulfilled. In early December, he wrote his secretary in Washington that he was about to cross the border at Laredo, adding cryptically, "I am going to Mexico with a pretty definite purpose which is not at present disclosable." Then, apparently traveling with Pancho Villa's rebel army, Bierce went to Chihuahua City, where he sent a Christmas Eve message to an acquaintance asking him to "pray for me—real loud." Two days later, a message to his secretary said he expected to head northward to observe the heavy fighting expected at Ojinaga. Bierce was never heard from again. But the end of his communiqués marked the beginning of speculation that continued for many years. Most historians believe he was the "old gringo" reportedly slain in the siege of Ojinaga, where Villa's insurgents burned the dead of both sides to prevent the spread of disease. Alternate theories abound, however. One suggests that he served as a spy in Mexico. Another claims that Pancho Villa himself admitted to having Bierce murdered for calling the rebels a band of thugs and threatening to switch his allegiance. Certainly, Villa had killed men for less. But Bierce's disappearance was also fertile ground for hoaxes. One persuaded Bierce's daughter that her father was alive and working for Lord Horatio H. Kitchener, England's war minister, and had seen action in the front lines in France. Unfounded rumors had him languishing in a California asylum and a suicide somewhere in the Grand Canyon. In 1932, a story circulated that he was being held captive in the same Brazilian Indian village where a Swiss trapper had seen a white man he thought was vanished British explorer Percy Fawcett *(page 8)*. "I like to think," wrote one biographer, "that Bierce ended up in some Andean village, laughing his head off." □

A Small Collectible

Six years after the disappearance of Ambrose Bierce, another Ambrose, named Small, mysteriously vanished in Canada. On December 2, 1919, Small accepted a check for one million dollars as partial payment for the sale of his Toronto-based theater chain, had his wife deposit the money, and, that evening, disappeared forever.

No one knows what happened to Ambrose Small. But at least one observer—the eccentric author Charles Fort—wondered about the curious coincidence of an Ambrose disappearing in Mexico and another vanishing in Canada a few years later. "Was somebody," Fort inquired, "collecting Ambroses?" □

The Russians Are Coming

The five-masted *Carroll A. Deering* appeared on North Carolina's treacherous Diamond Shoals early on the morning of January 31, 1921, driven aground with all sails set. Coast Guard rescuers were turned back by the ugly breakers but could still make out that the vessel "had been stripped of all life-boats and no sign of life on board." Another report said the ship looked "as if she had been abandoned in a hurry."

When, four days later, the seas subsided enough for Coast Guardsmen to board the 255-foot *Deering,* they found the ship empty and mortally stricken. Its hold was filled with water and its seams were ripped apart. No humans were aboard. So abruptly had the crew left that food was set out on the galley stove. For three weeks, the hulk sat on the reef while new storms blew; then it was dynamited as a hazard to navigation.

Almost at once, wild stories flew concerning the ship, which had been built in 1919 for the G. G. Deering Company of Portland, Maine, and named after a family scion. With a complement of twelve, the *Deering* had been plodding back unladen from Rio de Janeiro, with a single stop in Barbados. Subsequent investigations revealed that the ship's captain, W. T. Wormwell, had told a friend

that he mistrusted his crew, especially the first mate. Perhaps, some speculated, there had been a mutiny. The Coast Guard argued that the key to the *Deering* mystery was human panic. Disabled in a storm off the lower Carolina coast, the ship had appeared certain to hit the Diamond Shoals. The crew took to the lifeboats and soon perished in the rough seas.

There the matter might have rested. But a local resident claimed to have discovered a bottle washed up on a Carolina beach bearing a note from the vanished crew. As reported in the *New York Times,* the message read: "*Deering* captured by oil burning boat something like a chaser, taking off everything, handcuffing crew. Crew hiding all over ship. No chance to make escape. Finder please notify headquarters of *Deering.*" The *Times* claimed that the captain's wife had identified the ship's mate as the author. The troubling message raised the issue of piracy, to which the *Times* added an extra fillip. Conveniently ignoring *Deering's* empty holds, the paper con-

jectured that Bolshevik sympathizers were spiriting seized cargoes back to recently Communized Russia.

By itself, the *Deering* case might not have caused such wild speculation. But she was only one of many. The U.S. Department of Commerce revealed that little more than a week before the *Deering* was grounded, the steamer *Hewitt* had mysteriously vanished off Florida. The Italian steamer *Monte San Michele,* which left from New York for Gibraltar on February 2, 1921, disappeared, as did the British tanker *Ottawa,* which steamed from Norfolk, Virginia, on the same day and was last heard from on February 6. On February 3, the Brazilian freighter *Cabedello* left Norfolk for the Algerian port of Oran and was not heard from again. On the same departure date and from the same port, the British freighter *Esperanza de Larrinaga* set forth for Italy—and oblivion.

While the press had a field day totting up the disappearances, the most ominous suspicions came from government agencies. The State Department went on record as suspecting foul play in the *Deering* case and launched an investigation. The Department of Commerce had its own probe and was the first agency to raise the specter of Communist piracy. The hue and cry largely died away, however, when the man who claimed to have discovered the bottled message admitted he had forged it. And no connection was ever found to link the ill-fated *Carroll A. Deering* with the other lost ships—the vanished armada that haunts the stormy Carolina coastline. □

New York's Missingest Man

Joseph Force Crater was an ambitious, able lawyer who yearned to be remembered for his good works. When an opening occurred on the New York supreme court, Crater lobbied feverishly for it. In April 1930, Governor Franklin D. Roosevelt appointed the forty-one-year-old Crater to the high bench; however, to serve the full fourteen-year term, he would have to win a November election.

In June, Crater and his wife, Stella, headed for their Maine retreat. Some weeks later, on Sunday, August 3, Crater received a phone call that left him visibly upset. "I've got to straighten those fellows out," he told his wife. Then, promising to return for her August 9 birthday, he boarded the train for Manhattan.

Back in New York on Monday, August 4, Crater gave his live-in maid a few days off and saw his doctor about an index finger injured in a car door. On Tuesday, he worked in his chambers, and he spent much of Wednesday removing papers from his files. He had his assistant cash checks totaling $5,150 and, uncharacteristically, pocketed the money without counting it. Then he and the aide took the bundles of exhumed documents to Crater's Fifth Avenue apartment. That evening, Crater dined with show-business friends and, at about 9:15, hailed a taxi for the nearby theater district, hoping to catch the last act of a new drama entitled *Dancing Partner.* From the taxi he waved good-bye to his dining companions— and to the world.

When Crater did not return to Maine by August 9, Stella became concerned, even though this was not his first disappearance: He had once dropped out of sight for three weeks. She made some discreet inquiries, hoping to head off a scandal. But when Crater missed the opening of the supreme court session a few weeks later, his disappearance became sensational public knowledge.

Joseph Force Crater's missing-person dossier would grow to hundreds of pages as detective squads scoured the city and the state. But more than 300 interviews and thousands of letters, telegrams, and depositions failed to turn up a trace of Crater or the papers that he had taken from his files.

On the other hand, the investigation revealed much that Crater might have preferred kept quiet. The distinguished jurist had been entangled in a number of shady real estate and financial deals, and "Good old Joe Crater" had frequented Club Abbey, a ▷

Broadway speakeasy favored by mobsters. He had also indulged in a string of affairs with show girls and kept one long-term mistress.

A shaken Stella Crater finally returned to her Manhattan apartment on the last day of January 1931 and immediately made a startling discovery. Hidden in a secret bedside drawer was a manila envelope addressed to her in her husband's hand. It contained his will, which left everything to her, plus $6,619 in cash, several checks, stock certificates, bonds, life insurance policies, and a three-page note. Scrawled as if penned under great stress, the missive listed twenty-one people

who supposedly owed the judge money. The envelope had apparently been placed in the room after the police searches: Three of the checks were dated August 30, three weeks after Crater disappeared.

That was the last sign of Crater. The *New York Mirror* reported that he lived on in an isolated Mexican monastery. New York's police commissioner imputed no such high-mindedness to the missing justice but agreed that "Crater's disappearance was premeditated." After vanishing, Crater was "seen" driving a taxi in a dozen towns, panning for gold in California and Alaska, on trains and ships, and in a host of other incarnations.

But he may never have left Manhattan. One of the city's celebrated madams claimed that Crater suffered a fatal heart attack while gamboling in her establishment and thoughtful underworld friends had disposed of the body. Others told a still-seedier tale of intrigue and blackmail, culminating in Crater's being roughed up—and accidentally killed.

Though gone, Joseph Force Crater achieved his wish not to be forgotten. Dubbed the Missingest Man in New York, he became the butt of nightclub jokes ("paging Judge Crater . . .") and even entered the language: To pull a Crater *is* to vanish. □

A Vanished Justice

On the night of December 12, 1829, a hundred years before Joseph Crater was named to the bench, a former New York supreme court justice named John Lansing stepped out of his Manhattan hotel to post a letter on the Albany boat—and was never seen again. Historians speculate that enemies of the honest jurist had done him in. A biographer scoffed at such accounts, however, insisting that the judge had somehow fallen into the Hudson River and drowned—or had been robbed and murdered. □

Rush to Riches

One day in 1895, Massachusetts laborer Edward Rush had what was apparently his last argument with his wife. Enraged, he left the house without further explanation and disappeared. Thirty-five years later, on November 15, 1930, his wife and daughters responded to a knock on their door and found Rush back on their threshold. He declared that he had been "around the world many times. It's a tale out of the Arabian Nights." During his thirty-five years away, Rush had sought his fortune in the Orient and the South Seas—and had found it. Displaying handfuls of jewels and stacks of cash, he announced to his amazed family, "I am rich. You are rich." When asked why he had abandoned them, Rush replied unrepentantly, "I left on impulse and returned on impulse. It's that simple." □

Because It Is There

History credits New Zealander Sir Edmund Hillary and his Sherpa guide, Tenzing Norgay, as the first men to reach the summit of Mount Everest, 29,028 feet above sea level and the highest spot on the planet. Hillary and Tenzing set the official record in 1953, to universal acclaim. But some people believe that an Englishman had walked to the top of the world twenty-nine years earlier.

In late April 1924, a British schoolmaster named George Leigh Mallory began his second attempt to scale Everest. The thirty-seven-year-old Mallory had reconnoitered the Himalayan peak in 1921 and attempted an ascent in 1922, clad in the tweeds and hobnail boots that were the mountaineering gear of the day. But Chomolungma—the Goddess-Mother of the World, as Tibetans call the great mountain—had forced his party back with gale and avalanche. When asked why he tried Everest, Mallory is said to have made the immortal reply: "Because it is there."

Initially at least, his second assault proceeded smoothly. A series of seven camps were set up along the stone flank of the massif, and by the end of May, the climbers were ensconced in Camp IV, nearly 20,000 feet above sea level. On the morning of June 6, Mallory began a final two-day effort to reach the summit. With him were young Andrew Irvine as his partner and eight porters. Mallory selected Irvine, an inexperienced mountaineer, for his knowledge of the unwieldy apparatus that they used for breathing oxygen—dubbed "English air"—to augment the thin high-altitude atmosphere.

On June 8, having sent back their porters, Mallory and Irvine toiled on alone. An expedition member recalls peering that day through a telescope at two "black spots" inching upward toward the crest. They appeared to be on the final cliff face, the so-called Second Step, less than a thousand feet below the summit. But, as the colleague watched, the two men vanished in a snow squall.

Although neither man was ever found, no one doubts that Mallory and Irvine died upon the mountain. But some researchers think ◊

With climbing partner Andrew Irvine, George Mallory *(right)* disappeared near the top of then-unconquered Mount Everest in June 1924.

that Mallory very likely attained the prize before perishing in the cold.

Tom Holzel, a New England businessman and author, has made one attempt to retrace the steps of the ill-fated pair. He believes that Mallory pushed on ahead, sending the slower Irvine back toward camp and relative safety. Mallory would have kept Irvine's oxygen tank: Coupled with his own, it gave him a three-hour supply, just enough to reach the crest. He then worked his way along the final ledge, a narrow path flanked by 10,000-foot drops, aware that every labored upward step reduced his chances of returning alive. Holzel argues that Mallory made it before the blizzard killed him.

Irvine, meanwhile, must have lost his footing in fresh snow and fallen to his death on a terrace a thousand feet below. In 1979, a Chinese named Wang Hung Pao revealed to a party of fellow climbers that he had found the body of "an English" on that snow terrace during a 1974 climb. But the day after his curiously delayed disclosure, before his story could be corroborated, Wang himself perished in a crevasse and took the details of his find with him.

Holzel argues that Wang had found the body of Andrew Irvine. Subsequent crews have attempted to find the two climbers' remains and their equipment, especially their vest-pocket cameras. Preserved in the Himalayan ice, the film could be specially processed to bring out its sixty-six-year-old images. These could then be analyzed to see if any had been taken on the summit—and answer the nagging question of who was really first to conquer Everest. □

From Lae to Eternity

On July 2, 1937, a twin-engine Lockheed Electra thundered down a grass strip in Lae, New Guinea, so heavily laden with fuel that it barely cleared the rough ground at the end of the runway. Then, flying only a few feet above the ocean, it turned toward its next port of call, a coral pinpoint some 2,556 miles away. The Electra and its two-person crew were never seen again.

The pilot was Amelia Earhart— AE, as she liked to be called—at thirty-nine the best-known female flyer in the world. She had already flown the Atlantic alone, crossed the Gulf of Mexico, made the 2,400-mile run from Hawaii to California, and flown in scores of national aviation events. So much did she personify women in aviation that reporters, helped along by her publicity-minded publisher-husband, George Putnam, dubbed her Lady Lindy, a play on Charles Lindbergh's popular nickname.

By 1937, the only remaining challenge for Earhart was a flight around the globe at the equator. No other woman had yet circled the earth at any latitude, and no pilot had followed the long track through the tropics. "I have a feeling there is just one more flight in my system," AE told a friend. "This trip around the world is it."

Her companion and navigator on the long journey was forty-four-year-old Frederick Noonan, a pilot himself and arguably the best aerial navigator in the world. An adventurer in his own right, he had helped Pan American Airways pioneer its routes across the Pacific and flown as navigator on the first China Clipper flights from San Francisco to Manila. But a drinking

Shown here in a rare inflight photograph, Amelia Earhart's Lockheed 10-E Electra was specially modified to carry the extra fuel needed on the long legs of her 1937 round-the-world attempt.

problem had cost him his job and some reputation. For a largely reformed Noonan, the Earhart round-the-world flight was a crucial second chance.

On July 24, 1936, her thirty-ninth birthday, AE took delivery of NR-16020, a Lockheed 10-E Electra purchased for research by Purdue University, where Earhart was a visiting faculty member. Aided by Hollywood stunt pilot Paul Mantz, a close friend, Earhart had the Electra modified with large fuselage fuel tanks and radio-navigation gear, and she learned to fly this much bigger, more complex machine. However, by the time she began her first attempt in March 1937—a proposed 29,000-mile journey from California westward around the world—Earhart had only scant experience as an Electra pilot and almost no expe-

rience using newly developed radio-navigation techniques.

Trouble struck almost immediately. Following an uneventful flight from Oakland to Honolulu's Luke Field, Earhart's Electra was badly damaged on takeoff when it skidded around in a ground loop that wrenched away the landing gear, tore a wing, and bent both propellers. Several months later, when Lockheed finished rebuilding the wrecked plane, Earhart and Noonan set out again, this time from Oakland to Miami, following an eastward course dictated by seasonal weather changes in the tropics.

The first 22,000 miles of the journey went well, although, increasingly, AE slept poorly, ate little, and suffered nausea and diarrhea. Ignoring such discomforts,

she and Noonan winged above the Caribbean, South America, Africa, India, Burma, and Australia. By the time they reached New Guinea, however, both pilot and navigator showed signs of exhaustion.

Although they had only 7,000 miles to go, the 2,556-mile crossing from Lae to Howland Island was the most hazardous leg of all. A mile-and-a-half-long island that is difficult to find even with modern navigation equipment, Howland lay almost at the end of the Electra's range. The United States ◊

SAIPAN

The Many Final Flights of Amelia Earhart

TRUK — CAROLINE ISLANDS

Lae

NEW
GUINEA

THE INTENDED DIRECT FLIGHT from Lae to Howland Island should have put Amelia Earhart's Electra over that tiny strip of Pacific coral—and the Coast Guard cutter *Itasca*—by first light. But the plane never reached Howland, giving rise to a number of possible scenarios.

SPY THEORY A. Although there is no documentary evidence that Earhart and Frederick Noonan were on a secret mission, spy theories persist. In one, Earhart turned northwest to overfly the clandestine Japanese naval base at Truk, in the Caroline Islands, then, as night fell, headed for Howland Island. Near her destination, she broke radio silence to call the *Itasca*. But, believing Howland was behind her, she flew a series of north-south search tracks; then, lost and low on fuel, she turned toward the northwest, hoping to reach the Gilbert Islands. Instead, the Electra crash-landed at Mili Atoll in the Japanese-held Marshall Islands; Earhart and Noonan were either executed or sent to Japanese headquarters on Saipan, where they died as prisoners.

SPY THEORY B. Secretly flying a faster, longer-range military version of the Electra, AE followed one of several tracks. One would have taken her northward from Truk to reconnoiter Saipan, where she was forced down. Some say she and Noonan were executed there, while others think she survived him and was sent to Japan, then returned anonymously to the United States after the war.

In an alternative scenario, Earhart turned east at Truk and flew to the Marshall Islands, crashing at Mili, where she was captured, executed, or sent to Saipan.

The most elaborate scheme proposes that the disappearance was a ruse to let the U.S. Navy search for the missing plane in forbidden Japanese waters. After overflying Truk, Earhart flew on, made radio contact while near the *Itasca*, and then deliberately got lost, landing the Electra on the beach at tiny Canton Island, some 500 miles south of Howland. But the Japanese got there first and captured Earhart and Noonan.

WHAT REALLY HAPPENED? A close analysis of the flight by researchers Marie and Elgen Long of California indicates that Earhart must have come very close to her destination but thought she had flown past it. After flying a north-south search line, she ran out of fuel and was forced to ditch in heavy seas about 35 miles north and west of Howland Island, where she and Noonan perished.

ALL ISLANDS

MILI ATOLL

GILBERT ISLANDS

HOWLAND ISLAND

Itasca

CANTON ISLAND

UNITED STATES

Area of detail

Pacific Ocean

AUSTRALIA

Amelia Earhart waves to admirers near Londonderry, Northern Ireland, where she landed in 1932, the first woman to cross the Atlantic in an airplane.

government stationed naval ships along Earhart's route of flight and had the Coast Guard cutter *Itasca* anchored off Howland to provide help with its radio direction-finding gear. An experimental radio direction finder was set up on the island itself.

Midmorning on July 2, exhausted and jittery, AE and Noonan began the estimated twenty-hour flight to Howland Island. At 3:45 a.m. local time, about four hours before the Electra's estimated arrival time, Earhart made radio contact with the *Itasca*. Later, at 6:14, she requested a bearing—a compass heading to the ship. At 6:45, AE again requested a bearing. At 7:42, she came in once more: "We must be on you but cannot see you but gas is running low. Been unable to reach you by radio."

The *Itasca* beamed regular messages to the plane, but Earhart did not acknowledge receiving any until 8 a.m., when she again requested a bearing. As before, her transmission was too brief for the direction finders to pick up the Lockheed. When Earhart's voice came over the speaker at 8:44 it held a shrill note of apprehension. "We are on the line of position 157-337. . . . We are running north and south." The *Itasca* continued to monitor every radio channel the Electra might be using; but Amelia Earhart had sent her last message.

Within hours, the cutter and a small fleet of Navy ships were steaming north of Howland Island to begin the largest rescue attempt ever made for one airplane. Four thousand men in ten ships and sixty-five airplanes scoured 250,000 square miles of the Pacific in a sixteen-day search—and found nothing.

Already an international celebrity, Earhart swiftly became a prisoner of myth, and to some, an obsessing mystery. Theories of what really happened to Earhart and Noonan continued to sprout even half a century after they vanished over the Pacific.

One popular theory holds that the Electra headed north on a clandestine spy mission for the American government, to photograph and study the secret Japanese fortifications at Truk, in the Caroline Islands. Shot down or out of fuel, the doomed pair crash-landed in the Japanese-held Marshall Islands and were either executed or jailed. Eyewitness reports abound of two American pilots, one a woman, coming down in the Marshalls around 1937. But no corroborating evidence of capture has been discovered in American or Japanese archives.

Scrutinizing photographs of the Earhart Electra, some investigators have concluded that the accident at Honolulu's Luke Field was deliberate, permitting Lockheed to substitute a much faster military version of the Electra. They also claim that the pair survived both the crash and the imprisonment in Japan, and were secretly repatriated after the war, when they took up new, separate lives in the American northeast.

Most historians now believe the end was more mundane. Lost in bad weather, Earhart was forced to ditch the Electra in stiff winds and six-foot waves, a daunting prospect for someone who had never tried to put a heavy airplane down on the water before. If Earhart and Noonan survived the ditching, their situation would still have been perilous. The Electra's heavy engines would have made it float at a steep nose-down angle, the cabin underwater and the tail—along with the life raft stowed there—high in the air. And they might have had precious little time in which to act. In what appeared to be a textbook-perfect ditching in calm seas off Massachusetts, a similar Electra floated for only eight minutes.

After a painstaking study, two California researchers now believe they have narrowed Earhart's crash site to a rectangular area about 20 by 40 miles, some 35 miles west-northwest of Howland Island. There, they claim, in water more than two miles deep, a robot submersible should be able to locate the remains of NR-16020 and its lost crew, and finally lay the shades of Amelia Earhart and her navigator to rest. □

The Missing Swede

During the last year of the Third Reich, Nazi leaders began to force their "final solution" on the Jews of Hungary, the only large Jewish population remaining in Europe. But in Budapest, they unexpectedly encountered an effective adversary in the person of Raoul Wallenberg, a soft-spoken thirty-two-year-old Swedish gentile.

In 1944, when the U.S. War Refugee Board asked that a citizen from neutral Sweden undertake a rescue mission to help save the Jews of Hungary, young Wallenberg had volunteered, following his prominent family's tradition of public service. Once in Budapest and confronted with the magnitude of his task, he abandoned the conservative practices of his diplomatic colleagues. Instead, he freely distributed Swedish passports to at least 20,000 Budapest Jews, snatching many of them right off the deportation trains. He pulled people out of forced marches to the death camps and, when his supply of papers ran out, gave the dispossessed food, medical supplies, and clothing. He and his small staff sheltered some 13,000 Jews in houses protected by Swedish flags. Wallenberg prevented the massacre of 70,000 Jews herded into the Budapest ghetto by telling the commandant he would be hanged as a war criminal if he carried out Nazi orders to kill.

Wallenberg not only threatened—he also flattered, bribed, and cajoled, forged papers, and smuggled supplies. If it meant winning even temporary relief for his charges, he could dine amiably with Adolf Eichmann, the SS officer charged with exterminating Hungary's Jews.

On Christmas Eve, 1944, Soviet troops entered Budapest, opening what would become one of the war's bitterest sieges. On January 16, 1945, while the battle raged in the battered old city's streets, the Soviets announced that they had taken measures "to protect Mr. Raoul Wallenberg and his belongings." Wallenberg told a friend, "I don't know whether I am in custody or a guest."

On January 17, Wallenberg made a brief visit to the city's Swedish hospital and later stopped at one of the offices he had set up. There, he gave an assistant a wad of cash, explaining that he expected to be back in about eight days. Then, accompanied by his driver, a Russian officer, and two soldiers, he set out for the Soviet field headquarters at Debrecen, 120 miles to the east. Neither Wallenberg nor his driver ever returned. Apparently, for motives that are as obscure today as they were in 1945, the Russians had seized the Swede.

Despite official urgings to keep the matter quiet lest it ruffle Soviet sensibilities, the Wallenberg family pressed for information about the lost Raoul. In 1947, the Soviets said that the missing diplomat was "not known in the Soviet Union" and must have died in the battle for Budapest. But ten years later, repatriated prisoners released from Soviet camps spoke of encountering Wallenberg. Confronted with such stories, Russian authorities dug up a memorandum dated February 6, 1957, which said that Wallenberg had indeed been imprisoned in the Soviet Union but had died of heart failure in Moscow's Lubyanka prison on July 17, 1947. Still, in the late 1970s, ex-prisoners from various camps continued to report sighting Wallenberg, who would then have been near seventy. A Soviet doctor indicated that the Swede was living in a psychiatric ward. But there has been no authoritative account of Wallenberg's fate.

Hundreds of organizations worldwide have spoken out on behalf of Raoul Wallenberg. The United States made him an honorary citizen in 1981, and in the spirit of *glasnost*, the Soviets have reopened the case and Russian television has asked its viewers for any information they may have concerning Wallenberg's fate. Thus far, there has been only silence. □

This 1944 photograph of Raoul Wallenberg is thought to be the last taken of the Swede who saved thousands of Hungarian Jews from the Nazis.

Hitler's Minion

Said to be uneducated and brutish, Martin Bormann was nevertheless wily enough to become head of the Nazi party and Adolf Hitler's personal secretary. In the postwar era, Bormann has been, among a legion of missing Nazi war criminals, a perennial contender for the title of most wanted.

In April 1945, when the war in Europe had only a few weeks of bitter fighting still to go, Hitler, Bormann, and other members of the Nazi inner circle sought shelter in a Berlin bunker. There, as the end approached, Bormann witnessed Hitler's marriage to Eva Braun, signed Hitler's will, and helped preside over their cremation after the newlyweds committed suicide. Then, with a few others, Bormann left the stronghold under cover of night, huddled next to a tank for protection. His visible trail came to an end minutes later, when the tank ran into a deadly hail of Soviet fire.

The international war crimes tribunal at Nuremberg presumed that Bormann had survived and sentenced him to death *in absentia*. For years afterward, reports surfaced that Bormann had managed to escape his defeated fatherland. General Reinhard Gehlen, former chief of German intelligence for Soviet affairs, declared in 1971 that Bormann had been a Soviet spy even while in Hitler's service and that he had defected to the Soviet Union, where he subsequently died.

Other unsubstantiated sightings have had Bormann living under an alias as a jungle recluse in Colombia, as a carpenter in Guatemala, and as a Franciscan monk in Rome. In 1960, newspapers reported that a German-Jewish doctor in Argentina had recognized Bormann when he came in to be treated—and had given the Nazi a series of lethal injections.

In 1974, an American journalist asserted that Bormann had fled to Argentina in 1949 and claimed to have met the fugitive in a Bolivian hospital in the early 1970s. The reporter said that Bormann had fled Europe with the help of the Vatican and Argentine dictator Juan Perón, protected by a secret Nazi organization and a fortune smuggled out of Germany.

But Bormann may not have got that far from Hitler's bunker after all. In 1973, German authorities recovered a skeleton buried in West Berlin that, after extensive examination of the bones and dental work, forensic experts said belonged to Martin Bormann. Fragments of a glass vial found between its teeth suggested suicide by swallowing cyanide. As far as West German courts were concerned, that closed the Bormann case. For many others, however, he remains one of a dwindling number of aging Nazi war criminals who vanished nearly half a century ago and still remain at large. □

Martin Bormann, Hitler's private secretary and sinister shadow, confers with the Führer in February 1943.

Forever AWOL

At the United States Military Academy at West Point, visitors are closely monitored and tabs are kept on every student for virtually every minute of the day. Yet, Richard Calvin Cox, a second-year cadet, vanished from the academy's upstate New York campus on January 14, 1950, the first and, thus far, the last cadet to do so.

Cox was an unusually dedicated student. Ending high school in Mansfield, Ohio, as president of his class, he joined the army in 1946. He quickly rose to sergeant as a military policeman in occupied Germany and had the reputation of a sober and disciplined soldier. Once home from overseas, Cox fulfilled his long-time ambition of being appointed to West Point,

where he excelled in academics and in track.

Shortly after returning from Christmas break in his second year, Cox received a telephone call from someone named George, who said that he had known Cox in Germany. The cadet met his visitor later that day, seemed glad to see him, and signed out to accompany the newcomer to dinner at the nearby Hotel Thayer. Cox returned in less time than it would have taken to dine, however, and, uncharacteristically, fell into what his roommates described as a drunken sleep over his books. When the bugle tattoo call woke him at 10:30, he jumped up, startled and disoriented, and ran into the hallway shouting "Alice!" Later, he could not say why.

The next morning, Cox described with disgust the sadistic acts recounted by his visitor, who had boasted of emasculating German dead during the war and of hanging a pregnant girlfriend. Despite his obvious distaste, Cox met with the stranger again that afternoon. The next Saturday, January 14, Cox was seen talking to a civilian who looked something like George and that evening appeared in full-dress uniform to pick up his dinner pass.

When Cox did not meet his curfew, his roommates became concerned but waited until morning to notify authorities. When further investigation turned up no trace of the missing cadet, a massive search was launched. Ponds were drained, and soldiers on foot and in helicopters combed the academy grounds. Officials notified thirteen states and a number of em-

The 1950 disappearance of West Point cadet Richard Cox *(first row, far right)* from the academy grounds set off an unsuccessful worldwide search.

bassies abroad to be on the lookout for Richard Cox.

For nearly two decades afterward, investigators followed up hundreds of leads, which invariably turned into blind alleys. But no trace of Cox or of the man known only as George was ever found. Although the cadet's fate is still unknown, authorities have speculated that he might have been killed, or frightened into hiding, by someone with a grudge against a former military policeman. Perhaps, they say, something out of Cox's German experience had reached him, even behind the thick stone walls of West Point. □

Crabb Trap

The last time most of his friends saw Lionel "Buster" Crabb was in April 1956, just before he left his home in London for what he called a little job down in Portsmouth. He wrote his mother that the job would be easy and she shouldn't worry—but she should tear up the note. It was probably not the first time he had felt a need to reassure her. The tough, genial little man was Commander Crabb, the most famous British frogman of his day.

By the mid-1950s that day had largely waned. The Royal Navy had less need for an underwater hand and retired Crabb at forty-six. But diving remained his passion. He longed to "get m'feet wet again, get m'gills back," as he put it. Occasionally he would take off for Portsmouth Harbor for a few days, sorties that his acquaintances assumed were diving jobs for military intelligence.

Portsmouth was expecting other, more distinguished visitors that April. On the eighteenth, the 12,000-ton Soviet cruiser *Ordzhonikidze* and her destroyer escort were scheduled to arrive, bringing Marshall Nikolai Bulganin, the Soviet premier, and First Secretary Nikita Khrushchev to meet with British leaders.

Western naval experts had been eying *Ordzhonikidze* with interest, for she seemed unusually swift and agile. But the only way to find out if the Soviets were using a new type of hull or rudder would be to dip underwater and take a look. Officially at least, the British government banned any such provocative action, hoping to ease what were then strained relations with the Soviet Union.

On the morning before the Russians' arrival, Crabb checked into Portsmouth's Sallyport Hotel with a Mr. Smith. A day later, on the evening of the eighteenth, Crabb called his London office, as expected, and reportedly mused, "Well, I'm not as old as I thought"—a comment friends took to mean that he had gone diving.

Early on the morning of April 19, Crabb left the Sallyport. Later in the day, his fellow traveler, Smith, paid both bills, collected the commander's belongings, and disappeared.

When Crabb's friends began to make inquiries, naval officials advised them to keep quiet. A British intelligence officer from Portsmouth tore the April pages from the Sallyport register. A Soviet seaman had reported seeing a diver near his ship. As conflicting stories festered in the British press, spokesmen for the government stated that Commander Crabb had died while carrying out "frogman tests" in the Portsmouth area. However, "his presence in the vicinity of the [Soviet] destroyer occurred without any permission whatever and Her Majesty's government expresses their regret for the incident."

Some of Crabb's former colleagues thought that he must have been sent by an intelligence group to examine the hull of the Russian ships, as he had reportedly

done when the cruiser *Sverdlov* had called on Portsmouth six months earlier. Rumor held that he might have been freelancing for the American CIA and that the Soviets had detected and killed him. Some thought that he had been the victim of unsuitable diving gear. But no one admitted issuing Crabb orders, and no attempt was made to recover his body.

About a year later, a headless, handless corpse washed ashore twelve miles from Portsmouth. The body was wearing a frogman's suit of an Italian type Crabb favored and bore a scar like Crabb's on one knee. An inquiry determined that the remains were indeed those of Buster Crabb, and they were buried without official ceremony. But in 1959, a book by J. Bernard Hutton, a British journalist with East European contacts, told quite a different tale. Ostensibly based on a Soviet file, his story detailed the capture, interrogation, and imprisonment of the British diver—and Crabb's eventual decision to save his life by joining the Soviet navy as one Lvev Lvovich Korablov. A second Hutton book published in 1970 contained interviews of Soviets who claimed to have met Crabb, alleged messages from Crabb to his British fiancée, and descriptions of Lvev Korablov's career as a teacher of Soviet frogmen. But the British government still insists that the career of Buster Crabb ended beneath the murky waters of Portsmouth harbor more than thirty-five years ago. □

Michael Rockefeller, son of Governor Nelson Rockefeller, kneels among dancing Asmats, one of the primitive tribes he studied in New Guinea.

Death Takes the Heir

In 1960, newly graduated from Harvard, Michael Rockefeller joined a six-month expedition to film the natives of New Guinea's remote Baliem Valley. New Guinea was as raw a place as the world still offered: The 1,500-mile-long island, partitioned by impassably rough terrain, contained vast unexplored areas; among its hundreds of isolated ever-warring tribes, some remained untouched by civilization and practiced occasional head-hunting and cannibalism.

Searching out one's destiny in a stone-age land 15,000 miles from home was perfectly in character for the twenty-three-year-old adventurer. The son of New York governor Nelson Rockefeller and a third-generation heir to the Rockefeller oil fortune, he had become uncomfortable in his privileged life. As an alternative, he had spent summers working in a Puerto Rican supermarket and as a ranch

hand on his father's estate in Venezuela, and he had done his term in the U.S. Army Reserves as Private Rockefeller. The simple, timeless reality of New Guinea held a special fascination for him.

Half a year devoted to recording the customs of violent mountain tribes only whetted young Rockefeller's appetite for this dangerous, primitive existence. He went back to New York in September 1961 but returned almost immediately to New Guinea, this time to collect samples of the exquisite woodcarvings created by villagers along the southern Asmat Coast. There he was joined by René Wassink, a thirty-four-year-old Dutch anthropologist.

The two men had to travel from village to village by boat, along a nearly submerged shore of mangrove swamps, murky rivers, and tidal flats that people of the Asmat know as the "land of the lapping ◊

death." To transport the goods for which he was trading, Rockefeller used a forty-foot catamaran constructed from two dug-out canoes lashed together and driven by an eighteen-horsepower outboard motor. He had been warned that the underpowered craft was not equal to the force of the area's surging tides, but he apparently chose to ignore the advice.

On November 18, 1961, Rockefeller and Wassink set out from a Christian mission at Agats for Atsj, a village some 25 miles down the coast, their art-laden craft riding low in the water. Two local guides accompanied them. When they were several miles offshore and passing the mouth of the Eilanden River, a sudden tidal rip swamped the boat, drowning the engine and leaving the four helplessly adrift. As the improvised catamaran was drawn seaward, the two guides bravely dived into the rough, shark-infested waters, hoping to summon help. Rockefeller and Wassink remained with the boat. Soon, however, water was pouring in faster than the two men could bail; the canoes began to sink, then turned over.

Enduring one night of this, Rockefeller, who was a strong swimmer in peak condition, decided to try to make it to shore himself, using two empty fuel containers as floats. Wassink watched until Rockefeller's head and the two floats were mere dots on the sea. A Dutch flying boat, summoned by the alarms of the two guides, finally rescued the anthropologist, but Rockefeller was not found. The Dutch colonial government immediately set in motion a massive air, sea, and land search for the missing man. Natives were offered unimaginable wealth—250 sticks of tobacco—for any word leading to young Rockefeller's recovery. A gasoline can was finally found at sea but turned out not to be from the catamaran. A primitive world had absorbed Michael Rockefeller without a trace.

Most observers concluded that Rockefeller had been killed by sharks or saltwater crocodiles on his way to shore. But others are not so sure. Such incidents are extremely rare along the Asmat Coast, and the two guides had reached shore safely.

Many believe that Rockefeller made it to the beach, only to be destroyed by the fierce customs that had once drawn him. Even as the search for him began, rumors circulated in the jungle that a revenge killing called a payback had been carried out. A canoe bearing hunters of the ferocious Otsjanep tribe, four of whom had been killed not long before by Dutch officials, had come upon a white man in the water and killed him with their fish spears. Carrying the body ashore, the rumors said, they took the head as a trophy and ate portions of the remains before burying them in a shallow grave among the mangroves. □

Adrift

Early on July 10, 1969, the bridge crew of the Royal Mail Vessel *Picardy,* bound from London to the Caribbean, spotted a small sailing yacht some 700 miles southwest of the Azores. The forty-one-foot craft—a three-hulled design called a trimaran—was making only about two knots in calm seas, with just a mizzen sail spread. When loud blasts of a foghorn failed to produce any response, a boarding party was sent to explore. They found the sails neatly furled, the life raft still secured on deck, and no evidence of an accident. In the untidy cabin, three radios had been dismembered in an apparent effort to repair them, the sink was filled with dirty dishes, and on one of the tables, a set of blue logbooks had been carefully arranged. But of thirty-seven-year-old Donald Crowhurst, the lone skipper of the *Teignmouth Electron,* they discovered no trace.

The trimaran had left Teignmouth, Devon, on October 31, 1968, competing in the first nonstop, solo sailing race around the world, sponsored by the *Times* of London. Because the nine entrants were allowed to choose their sailing time between June 1 and October 31, 1968, the Golden Globe race offered a five-thousand-pound prize for the fastest journey and a

When the three-hulled *Teignmouth Electron* was found in the Atlantic, on July 10, 1969, only its mizzen sail was set *(left)*. Its captain, Donald Crowhurst *(below)*, was mysteriously gone.

trophy for being first. When found by the *Picardy*, the *Teignmouth Electron* was only about 1,800 miles from home and a certain winner of at least one of the prizes. The first of Crowhurst's logs seemed to verify this; but another told quite a different story.

The race had begun badly for Crowhurst. An electronics engineer with a failing business, he had hit upon competing as a way of publicizing a navigation aid he had designed and had outfitted his one-of-a-kind vessel with a variety of automated gear. But this left many technical bugs to be worked out before October 31, the last day contestants could begin the race. As Crowhurst sailed out of the harbor that autumn day in 1968, his supplies had yet to be stowed, and loose wires and unassembled equipment lay strewn about the boat. And he had no detailed course worked out—just the rough outlines of the 30,000-mile voyage and a collection of charts.

Within two weeks, his troubles had multiplied. The boat leaked and the pumps were not hooked up properly, so he had to bail; the electrical generator had given out; and the sails required rerigging. In his log, the worried skipper agonized over whether to continue.

After three weeks, however, Crowhurst began to keep two separate accounts. One was a dream log, in which he recorded the distances and adventures a successful racing sailor would like to have had. This log and the reports he radioed to his press agent showed him zipping around the globe at 170 miles and more a day, describing imagined sea and weather conditions.

The other log was precise, de- ◊

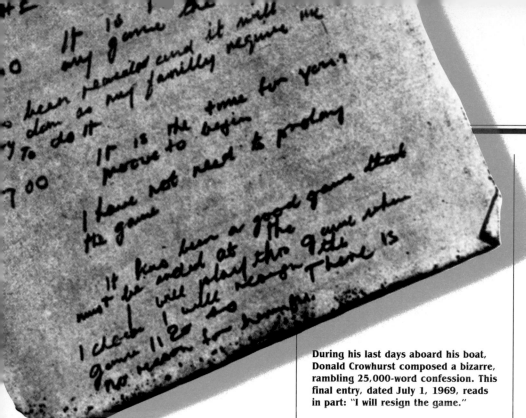

During his last days aboard his boat, Donald Crowhurst composed a bizarre, rambling 25,000-word confession. This final entry, dated July 1, 1969, reads in part: "I will resign the game."

tailed, depressing, and probably true. There Crowhurst recorded daily runs sometimes as short as 13 miles and a host of tribulations. Rather than a round-the-world dash, this log described a voyage to South America, including a clandestine call at a remote port for repairs, then weeks of marking time off the coast of Argentina. Although he had covered nearly 17,000 miles, he had never left the Atlantic.

Finally, as he turned back toward England, Crowhurst's conscience had begun to torment him. He had apparently hoped to time his return so as to have no chance of winning—and no detailed scrutiny of his voyage. But an ironic turn doomed him to success. One boat had completed the voyage, and seven others had, for various reasons, dropped out of the race. Now, hearing that Crowhurst was close behind him, the only remaining contestant pushed his boat too hard in an Atlantic storm and sank her. To Crowhurst, the news meant

certain success and great publicity. Instead of returning to England a valiant loser, he must go home a triumphant fraud. On June 25, he made his last radio transmission; then, cut off from the world, he abandoned the shipboard work he called sailorizing and began writing a 25,000-word amalgam of confession and philosophy that became steadily more bizarre and incoherent. The ramblings trailed off with the entry for July 1, 243 days after he had set to sea: "I will resign the game 11-20-40. There is no reason for harmful . . ."

Some maintain that his agonized derangement was feigned and that he somehow went ashore in the Azores or South America. And there is the more mundane possibility that Crowhurst, who had a reputation for clumsiness on deck, may have slipped and fallen overboard. More likely, the would-be circumnavigator "resigned" by stepping off the trimaran's stern into the sea, to watch helplessly as she sailed on without him. □

Airline Pirate

Shortly after Northwest Airlines flight 305 took off from Portland, Oregon, on Thanksgiving eve in 1971, a man in a business suit and dark glasses coolly handed a cabin attendant a note that claimed his briefcase contained a bomb and warned "no funny stuff." In Seattle, he exchanged the thirty-six passengers and most of the crew for $200,000 in $20 bills and four parachutes. Then he told the pilot of the Boeing 727 to take off again. This time the plane headed for Reno, Nevada, with its landing gear and flaps extended and the cabin unpressurized. Close to their destination, the flight deck crew saw a light signal indicating that the rear exit stairs had been extended. When they checked, they discovered that the airplane was empty. The man who had bought his ticket under the name of Dan Cooper—a reporter later called him D. B. Cooper, which stuck— had disappeared somewhere along the mountainous route.

FBI agents believe that the lightly clad thief, who bailed out at an altitude of 10,000 feet into freezing rain, howling wind, and subzero temperatures, probably died in the jump. If Cooper survived it at all, they say, he most likely landed injured, to perish in the wilderness.

The only skyjacker of a domestic aircraft in American history to elude capture, Cooper became a northwestern folk hero. Residents remembered him immediately when, in 1980, an eight-year-old boy discovered a bundle of $20 bills washed up on the muddy banks of the Columbia River near Portland, Oregon. The serial numbers of the bills matched those given to Dan Cooper in Seattle nine years earlier; but those were the only bills of the air pirate's 10,000 twenties to turn up.

There have been some tantalizing clues about Cooper's fate. In 1974, for example, escaped convict Richard Floyd McCoy was gunned down in a shootout with pursuing FBI agents in Pennsylvania. A former Sunday-school teacher and Green Beret helicopter pilot, Mc-Coy had been serving a forty-five-year sentence for skyjacking a United Airlines jet for $500,000. Floyd's technique had been virtually identical to Cooper's, down to the phrase "no funny stuff" in his note and his parachuting out of the airplane. When captured and asked if he were indeed the vanished Cooper, McCoy refused to say. But years of research led two investigators to conclude that Mc-Coy and Cooper were one and the same man. In fact, photos of Mc-Coy and reconstructed images of Cooper show a strong, although inconclusive, resemblance. But the elusive Cooper's end may have been gentler than McCoy's. A woman identified only as Clara has claimed that Cooper, calling himself Paul Cotton, limped into her life with a broken ankle back in 1971, and he happily stayed with her until his death from illness eleven years later. □

The only sign ever found of skyjacker "D. B. Cooper"—shown here as depicted by a police artist—was some twenty dollar bills from his ransom money (background), discovered on a riverbank.

Lucky Lord

On November 7, 1974, the usual Thursday-night festivities at the Plumber's Arms, a pub in London's fashionable Belgravia District, were interrupted when a small, brown-haired woman rushed in, her head streaming blood. "He's murdered the nanny," she screamed. "The children are in the house. . . . He's in the house." Then Veronica, countess of Lucan, collapsed.

When the police arrived at the Lucan house at 46 Lower Belgrave Street, they found the basement kitchen in darkness and the room and stairs spattered with blood. The horribly bludgeoned corpse of Sandra Rivett, a nanny hired four weeks before, had been stuffed into a canvas mail sack. A length of lead pipe wrapped in bloodstained adhesive tape was discovered in an adjoining room. In the morning, the hospitalized countess told police that "he" was her estranged husband, Richard John Bingham, the seventh earl of Lucan. He had apparently murdered Sandra Rivett by mistake, Lady Lucan declared. Then, discovering he had killed the wrong woman, he had waited in ambush for his wife. When she came downstairs, she said, he tried to kill her. But her determined resistance held him off, and he fled into the night.

At about the time Lady Lucan swept into the Plumber's Arms, a disheveled Lord Lucan, driving a borrowed car, dropped in on old friends in Uckfield, Sussex, forty-four miles away. Fortified with whiskey, he wrote several letters about what he called "a traumatic night of unbelievable coincidence." According to Lucan, he had been observing his wife's house—he did

this obsessively, hoping to find some lever with which to regain custody of his children—when he had seen an intruder in the basement kitchen struggling with a woman he believed was Veronica. He ran to the rescue, let himself in with his own key, and tried to get to the assailant, but slipped on a pool of blood and fell before he could stop the killer. "The circumstantial evidence against me is strong, in that [Veronica] will say it was all my doing," he wrote. "I will lie doggo for a while." He left his friends' home after one o'clock and was not seen again.

On the afternoon of Sunday, November 10, police found the car Lucan had been driving parked in the port city of Newhaven. The interior was stained with blood of uncertain origin, and a second length of lead pipe wrapped in tape was discovered in the trunk. The car had been there since early Friday morning.

For the British press, the story of the thirty-nine-year-old peer of the realm was sensational in the extreme, involving not only a brutal murder but also the dark underside of an aristocratic life. Lord Lucan, it seemed, was a thoroughgoing anachronism. His politics and manner were those of his great-great-grandfather, who had ordered the Light Brigade's fatal charge at Balaclava during the Crimean War. Trapped in the past, Lucan led a narrow existence of small talk, dining, and gambling at the patrician clubs of London.

But the man nicknamed Lucky Lucan squandered his family money, saw his marriage turn sour, and watched his luck run out on the gambling cloth at the exclusive Clermont Club. He had tried unsuccessfully to have Veronica committed to a mental hospital before their 1973 separation, which was followed by a bitter, expensive custody fight that Lucan lost. Increasingly morose, drinking heavily, and obsessed about his children, he spiraled downward.

After the crime, police scoured Lucan's address book, speaking with more than ninety reticent witnesses. (Members of the upper-class "Lucan set" were not eager to discuss a friend in trouble). No trial for the slaying of Sandra Rivett was ever held, but the inquest named Lucan as her killer.

Every November brings a new flood of "sightings" of the missing peer—in Africa, Brazil, France, and England—but even his most supportive friends doubt that he could long endure outside his soft world of privilege. More likely, his dread of a trial and conviction drove him into the sea off Newhaven. "He was a warrior, a Roman," his friend John Aspinall, former owner of the Clermont Club, told a Bristish writer. "He was quite capable of falling on his sword, as it were." Still, nearly two decades later, Lady Lucan has not asked that her husband be declared legally dead. □

The Hoffa Hit

James Riddle Hoffa ruled the International Brotherhood of Teamsters from 1957 to 1971, transforming it into the world's largest, richest, and possibly most corrupt trade union. From 1967 onward, he ran the union from a prison cell, convicted of jury tampering and fraudulent use of pension funds.

The union's vice president, Frank Fitzsimmons, helped convince President Richard Nixon to grant Hoffa a conditional release on parole in 1971. The condition: Hoffa could not hold union office until 1980. Unaware of this restriction until after his release, Hoffa said Fitzsimmons had double-crossed him and sought to have the prohibition lifted. A power struggle for the Teamster presidency began. On July 30, 1975, Jimmy Hoffa drove

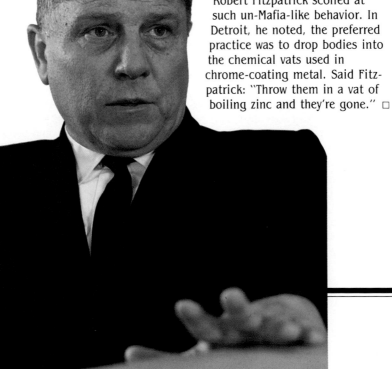

into Detroit from a summer home in Lake Orion for a business lunch at the Machus Red Fox, a restaurant in suburban Bloomfield. He apparently expected to sit down with powerful gangland figures and solicit their support. They never showed up, he told his wife a few hours later on the telephone. The sixty-two-year-old labor leader was last seen driving away from the restaurant with several other men.

Most believe Hoffa was murdered by the Mob. But his body has never been found, even though tips have led investigators to dig up fields, rip up cement floors, and drag rivers. In 1982, a Justice Department informer alleged that Fitzsimmons had preempted Hoffa's plan to kill him, and the assassins had ground up the remains and dumped them in a swamp. Self-styled freelance hitman Donald Frankos said in 1989 that Hoffa's shredded remains had been stored in a freezer, then interred in concrete during construction of the Giants football stadium in New Jersey. Former FBI official Robert Fitzpatrick scoffed at such un-Mafia-like behavior. In Detroit, he noted, the preferred practice was to drop bodies into the chemical vats used in chrome-coating metal. Said Fitzpatrick: "Throw them in a vat of boiling zinc and they're gone." □

Jim Thompson sits with his cockatoo in the good times before his disappearance in Malaysia.

The Silk King

A veteran of America's wartime Office of Strategic Services, Jim Thompson had first come to Bangkok after World War II as an intelligence officer, and the Orient had captivated him completely. Thompson also found a business opportunity in Thailand. The tradition of weaving iridescent silk was in decline, but he sensed that the fabric might be popular in Western markets. His hunch was correct, and Thompson transformed the moribund silk-weaving trade into a multimillion dollar export industry.

As manager of the Thai Silk Company, he built a magnificent Thai-style mansion to display his extensive art collection, which he opened part of the time to tourists. The splendid company and fare at the Thompson table attracted such celebrities as writer Somerset Maugham, politician Adlai Stevenson, and singer Ethel Merman, among many others.

On March 26, 1967, Thompson was visiting friends in the Malaysian resort of Cameron Highlands. Following an Easter picnic lunch, the party of four retreated to their cottage for an afternoon nap. His friends later said that they thought he had sat on the lawn while the others slept inside. When, shortly after three o'clock, they heard what sounded like someone walking down the gravel drive to the road, they assumed it was Thompson going for a stroll. They never saw their friend again.

Because Thompson left behind two items that he carried virtually everywhere—his cigarettes and his pills prescribed to ease the pain of gallstones—his companions assumed that he had just gone out to stretch his legs and subsequently had become lost in the jungle. However, a search party of residents, soldiers, dogs, local aborigines, and psychics failed to find any trace of him in the nearby forest. If Thompson had perished after falling into a ravine or an animal trap, or if he had been killed by a tiger, vultures would have congregated overhead, but none were seen. One Asian hand who knew the local jungle people well and questioned them closely became convinced that Jim Thompson was nowhere in the area.

The rumors began where the search party left off. It was said that the Thai silk king had been kidnapped for political reasons or that he had been forced into secret exile by his alleged CIA connections. Some people speculated that Thompson had been kidnapped for money, but no ransom demands ever surfaced.

Thompson's friends have acknowledged that he could have been trapped in a net that he himself had spun. "He embroidered stories," said one. "He let people wonder whether he might or might not be a spook. Actually, he wanted them to believe it. It made him larger than life." It is possible that Jim Thompson's innocent innuendo of intrigue resulted in his execution as a spy. □

An Atmosphere of Mystery

In 1983, an international group of scientists announced that a nuclear war might be followed by something even worse: nuclear winter, a lethal, worldwide freeze caused by airborne debris blotting out the sun. One of the scientists involved in the ensuing debate was physicist Vladimir Valentinovich Alexandrov, the brilliant forty-six-year-old director of a Soviet climatic research laboratory in Moscow.

In some circles, Alexandrov had already acquired a kind of celebrity. A frequent, freewheeling visitor to the United States, he had in 1978 been allowed to solve climate equations on Cray supercomputers in Colorado—machines powerful enough to simulate the complexity of the atmosphere and to perform such dense calculations as those used in nuclear weapons design. As the only Soviet scientist with access to an American supercomputer, Alexandrov acquired immense prestige at home. But he also attracted the interest of American security agencies. When further research convinced most sci-

entists that the apocalyptic nuclear winter would actually be a more tolerable nuclear autumn, Alexandrov stubbornly clung to the more sensational view. In official American eyes, his behavior became less that of scientist than of someone bent, as one western colleague expressed it, on "putting the Soviets on the side of the angels." In January 1985, U.S. officials marked his passport with a note forbidding further access to American supercomputers, and he had trouble getting his American visa renewed. In March, a Pentagon report branded him a Soviet propagandist who used obsolete science to make an ideological point.

Although Soviet officials must have been dismayed by Alexandrov's loss of status, they nevertheless allowed him to travel once more—this time to speak at an international conference in Spain. However, upon arriving in Madrid on March 29, he was whisked away to the Soviet embassy for half an hour. No one who knows will say what transpired there, but accord-

ing to his Spanish driver, Alexandrov emerged a different man. The humorous, charismatic, self-controlled scientist known to American colleagues seems to have vanished, to be replaced by a determinedly self-destructive drunk. Alexandrov went on a binge in Madrid, and later that evening, in Córdoba, where his talk was scheduled for the next morning. After delivering a lackluster paper at the conference, Alexandrov went off on another drinking spree that saw him stagger from a cab to his hotel at three the next morning. A few hours later, he was on his way to Madrid, and although he did not know it, to the Soviet embassy. Eyewitness reports contradict each other at this point, but it appears that Alexandrov panicked when he realized that his driver meant to take him to the embassy and tried to escape on foot. Embassy officials caught him, shepherded him into a van, and sent him to Madrid's Hotel Habana.

Alexandrov left the hotel around eleven that night, acting inebriated. The hotel attendant said that even later in the night, Alexandrov tried to enter a nearby bingo parlor, requesting wine. He was ushered out, tried to return, and was escorted out again. That is the last confirmed sighting of Alexandrov.

Colleagues and the U.S. press speculated that the physicist had either defected, been assaulted in a dark Madrid street, or gone underground in Europe. Some believe that Soviet agents assassinated the out-of-favor scientist. No official comment has come from either side. But the Madrid police say they have received not "one bit of pressure" from the Soviet Union to search for Alexandrov. □

Wallflower

When Manuel Cortes, the mayor of the Spanish village of Mijas, vanished in March 1939, it seemed to have little effect on his family. Their lives went on imperturbably, while efforts by both friends and the police failed to turn up any trace of Manuel.

As mayor, Cortes had organized free education for all and parceled out some of the larger estates to landless laborers. During the bitter 1936-1939 Spanish Civil War, he had sided with the Loyalists against the Nationalist rebels of General Francisco Franco. But after Franco's victory, Cortes found himself marked for execution because of his wartime sympathies.

Instead of absconding ahead of the firing squad, the thirty-four-year-old Cortes disappeared into a hollow space between two walls of his foster father's house, which he entered through a hole concealed by a large picture. Thereafter, he spent his days in that cramped space, sitting on a child-size chair, eating what his wife, Juliana, secretly brought for him in a covered basket. He emerged only after night had fallen.

Juliana developed several small businesses to support Manuel and their daughter: distributing eggs, drying coarse grass for making sacks, and operating taxicabs. Thanks to her earnings, the family moved to their own house. Juliana smuggled Manuel through the streets after midnight, disguised as an old woman. Through his long, self-imposed disappearance, Cortes spent his time reading, listening to the radio, and helping Juliana dry the grass and keep the books. From his hiding place, he could look out a peephole to the street below. When his daughter married, he watched her wedding through a keyhole.

On March 28, 1969—thirty years after his exile began—he heard by radio that Franco was pardoning political offenders from the civil war. After official confirmation of his pardon, the aging radical emerged into the sunlight for the first time in three decades. □

One of the uni-
versal properties
of things is a tenden-
cy to vanish into a virtual land of the lost.
Currencies and coins disappear into piggy
banks and penny jars; public conveyances fill
with odd residual belongings. Time, and time
capsules, may be lost, and so may the fossil
remains of earlier races whose various pos-
sessions, no doubt, also sometimes disappeared. Artistic masterpieces, doomed by
chemistry, flake away into oblivion, and what
the postman cannot deliver goes to grave-
yards for lost mail.
Even places and their
postmarks are ephemeral.

Some psychologists believe that people
lose mostly what they want to, such as the
bitter spouse who habitually misplaces an un-
consciously hated wedding ring. But people
also lose those things they most cherish; psychology aside, lost things are often simply
lost, sometimes forever. Still, now and then,
a vanished object will follow an improbable
course back to its owner. Carelessness and bad
luck do not always have the last word.

Purloined Letters

In the spring of 1585, a postal courier left Milan, Italy, bound for Cologne, Germany, with a batch of nearly three hundred letters addressed to recipients in Germany, Belgium, and the Netherlands. The mail shipment traveled safely through Switzerland and into Germany but somehow disappeared before reaching its destination.

Then in 1889, when the law courts in Frankfurt—about a hundred miles southeast of Cologne—were moving to a new building, the vanished mail shipment turned up among papers in the cellar. Although the find was a boon to scholars, who were able to examine the three-hundred-year-old correspondence, it shed little light on why the mail had gone astray in the first place. Most of the letters were in Italian. Some admonished students to study harder for their German exams, while in others merchants complained to Dutch suppliers. Many simply ordered various kinds of merchandise for customers in Milan.

Missing, however, were messages from the politically and ecclesiastically powerful of the day, an odd omission considering the tumultuous religious situation in 1585. Gebhard Truchsess, Catholic archbishop and Elector of Cologne, had defected from the Church, and the Rhineland was shuddering under frequent riots.

Scholars have suggested that the courier was robbed in what was then rough hill country about thirty-five miles north of Cologne on the Rhine River. A similar mail robbery had occurred there twenty-four years earlier. Some historians believe the hijacking was staged by postal officials as an act of revenge against their own postmaster in Cologne. Others concluded that the robbery was politically motivated, intended to intercept a piece of official mail that someone—perhaps the archbishop himself—did not want to reach Cologne. But the real motive for the disappearance, and how the stolen letters made their way to Frankfurt, will probably never be known. □

This letter was one of a packet that surfaced mysteriously three hundred years after being mailed from Milan.

A Lost Card

On September 22, 1918, just seven weeks before the end of World War I, George Kemp mailed a postcard from the trenches in France to Donald Templeton, his nine-year-old nephew back home in Buffalo, New York. Kemp was killed in the final weeks of fighting, and his message to the boy seemed to disappear. Then, on July 6, 1981, the 63-year-old missive was finally delivered to its Buffalo address. Kemp's relatives had long since moved away, but the new residents managed to trace the 72-year-old Templeton to his home in Florida, where they forwarded his late uncle's posthumous greetings.

Postal authorities believe that the card spent years wedged in the back of some piece of furniture or equipment, remaining undiscovered until its hiding place was scrapped. At the time that it was found, according to normal postal-service procedure, the card should have received a special stamp explaining the delay in delivery. No one is quite sure why that did not occur in this case.

Nor can anyone explain the mystery of the card's multiple postmarks. It was first stamped by a military censor in France, then with a 1918 cancellation mark. At later stages in its prolonged journey, the card received two additional postmarks—one in 1927, the other in 1981, just a few days before its delivery. The first and last postmarks are perfectly understandable, but nobody knows what happened in 1927. It seems that the card disappeared once, resurfaced briefly nine years later, then vanished again for more than half a century. □

Zapped Zips

Every year, between 150 and 200 American towns disappear—at least as far as the U.S. Postal Service is concerned. Driven by rising or falling population figures, post offices are established and discontinued as people migrate into and out of communities across the land. Most of the closed facilities are in rural areas, and in the western and the southern states. Often, a shutdown occurs because no one can be found to act as postmaster or there is no landlord willing to accommodate a post office.

Communities can appeal the closing of their local post office (and their being shuffled into a nearby zip code), but the process often takes eighteen months to percolate through the system, and appeals are not always successful. The best way to bring a vanished post office back is to increase the area's population, and thus its vol-

ume of mail. In the mountains of Kentucky and West Virginia, for example, a reopened coal mine can resuscitate a community and put it back onto the postal map. □

The post office at Whiteside Cove, North Carolina, opened in 1878, became Grimshawes post office in 1909, and canceled its last stamps *(above)* **in 1953. Former postmaster Warren S. Alexander stands in front of the structure.**

Wayward Parts and Parcels

Every year the dead-parcel offices of the U.S. Postal Service handle more than a million packages that can be neither delivered nor returned to sender, owing to missing, illegible, or incorrect addresses. Lost between sender and recipient, the undeliverable parcels contain everything from excrement to precious gems. Quantities of illegal drugs find their way to these postal cemeteries, along with a rich variety of lost items as exotic as human organs and live animals,

as mundane as home furnishings and parts for automobiles. Greg Hawthorne, head of the dead-parcel office in St. Paul, Minnesota, has said, "We figure we could put a car together in about two years with all the various car parts we get in lost packages."

In fact, lost goods do not stay around long enough to be assembled into working machines or otherwise enjoyed by postal workers. Illegal or suspect material, such as drugs and pornography, is forward-

ed to the U.S. Postal Inspector. Books and recordings that cannot be delivered are shipped back to their producers. Other valuables are normally sold at periodic postal-service auctions. On one occasion in the 1930s, the contents of an undeliverable package were deemed too good for the block, however: a box filled with hundreds of drawings by the eighteenth-century English artist George Romney. Unable to identify the sender or addressee, postal ◊

officials turned in the art treasures to the U.S. Library of Congress.

A dead-parcel office can be a disconcerting place to work. Employees in New York and Atlanta recall packages containing live snakes. A crate full of human eyeballs ended up at the St. Paul facility, because the medical lab to which it was addressed had gone out of business. The same office received one parcel containing a pig's severed head and another with a dead rat crammed full of opium. An accompanying note read: "Happy birthday, you dirty rat. Enjoy the opium." □

Part of six weeks' undeliverable mail from the American northeast languishes at the U. S. Postal Service's dead-parcel office in New York City.

Vanishing Checks

Tellers in a number of Tennessee, Indiana, and Illinois banks could not help noticing the peculiar odor and the wet, oily feel of certain checks that they received for deposit. When asked about the unpleasant texture and smell, the depositors explained that they had dropped the checks in snow or puddles of water.

In fact, the greasy bank drafts had been soaked in a chemical that caused them to disintegrate into ashlike scraps within about twelve hours of being treated. A few days later, the crooked depositors would withdraw the money that had been credited to their accounts from the disappearing checks and disappear themselves. The scam was also used to fleece merchants, who found themselves selling merchandise for checks that subsequently

vanished, taking all evidence of the transaction with them.

Between December 1987 and February 1988, criminals used at least eighteen vanishing checks to scoop up an estimated $50,000 to $80,000. Most of the fraudulent checks disappeared while nobody was looking, fragmenting invisibly inside a teller's drawer or in an armored transport en route from bank to check processing center. But at least one check dissolved

before the eyes of a startled bank employee who described the paper curling at the edges like ancient parchment, then falling apart like a crumbling cracker. This, and the occasional failure—some checks disintegrated only partially— brought the swindle into view.

Until then, the scheme had succeeded because of the procedure that banks follow with check deposits. The money is credited to the depositor's account but cannot be withdrawn for several days while the check travels to a processing center to be cleared, if valid, or bounced back to the bank if not. If, however, the check disappears before reaching the processing center, nothing is ever returned to the bank, which, at the end of the waiting period, automatically releases the funds for withdrawal.

Although police and federal agents had their suspicions, they made no arrests. And if police chemists have isolated the substance, they are not talking. □

Chicago police captain James Zurawski flourishes a novel breed of rubber check: A secret chemical treatment causes the worthless draft to disintegrate before it bounces.

Italy Unchanged

When the Italian small-change coins *spiccioli* began to vanish in 1965, some said the lightweight aluminum pieces were being collected by the Japanese for cheap watch cases. Others thought the coins were disappearing into cloth-covered buttons or, perhaps, simply blowing away.

In fact, the disappearance of spiccioli began in 1964 when, faced by soaring double-digit inflation, the Italian government ceased minting the silver 500-lira piece, which had become more valuable as metal than as money. Italians were expected to make change with smaller aluminum coins worth 5, 10, 20, 50, 100, and 200 lire. But the national supply of small change was swiftly devoured by coin-operated vending machines, by tourists going home with pocketfuls of nearly worthless foreign coins, and by work stoppages at the Italian mint.

As a result, getting change while shopping became a major problem. The post office tried to solve it by giving out stamps worth a few *centesimi* (100 to the lira), but a huge envelope was needed to accommodate the numerous stamps required even for local delivery.

Butchers passed out eggs as a fragile alternative to coins. News vendors, given 100-lira pieces for 90-lira newspapers, made change with candy valued at 10 lire, and many storekeepers dealt out such differences in the form of nougat and licorice.

The use of sweets as coinage led Senator Augusto Premoli to sponsor legislation that would have the Italian mint print candy wrappers in the denominations of the missing coins. His bill was voted down, but many banks went ahead on their own, printing a kind of mini-check in the amount of the vanished lira pieces. Actually worthless bits of paper, these were accepted by merchants and have since become collectors' items, trading for far more than their minuscule face value.

Not until 1976 did the tide begin to turn. Then, a new 200-lira coin was introduced, followed in 1978 by a nonsilver 500-lira piece. With this infusion of new coins, the famine of small change quickly turned into an embarrassment of small-denomination riches. □

Missing Money

Billions of dollars worth of U.S. coins and bills disappear from circulation annually—more than $70 million in pennies alone in a typical year. Some of this vanished money simply gets lost, or is worn out, added to collections, or squirreled away in cookie jars and piggy banks. Some of it languishes forgotten in the pockets of unworn clothing or lurks in the obscure corners of handbags, upholstery, drawers, and closets. But much of it slips away into a shady labyrinth of international finance designed to evade taxes and "launder" illicitly earned money, making it seem to have a legitimate source. This practice is so pervasive that U.S. Treasury officials estimate they can physically locate only about 20 percent of the bills they print. Much of the remaining 80 percent presumably disappears into the global laundering apparatus. □

Watery Wallets

Vermont native Randy Lindquist *(below)* was deep-sea fishing off the New England coast in the summer of 1989 when his wallet dropped overboard and sank into the Atlantic, seemingly lost forever. But a week later, another deep-sea angler, Dennis Murphy, reeled in the wallet twenty miles north of the spot where it went into the water, at a depth of only 125 feet. When Murphy returned the wallet to its owner, its $93 in cash and credit cards were intact. Said Lindquist, "I had better odds hitting the Megabucks lottery than ever seeing that wallet again."

The odds against Robert Howley's recovering his wallet were even longer. He lost his while trolling for fish in New Hampshire's Lake Winnipesaukee in 1985 and thought the wallet and the $480 it contained were gone. The loss provoked frequent teasing from his friends. So, when a stranger named Robert Ouellette telephoned in 1989 to say he had recovered the wallet, Howley thought at first the caller was joking. He soon discovered, however, that Ouellette was perfectly serious. Scuba-diving in search of an antique boat's lamp, he had come upon the wallet some 200 yards offshore in 30 feet of water. Howley retrieved the waterlogged wallet, $480 in well-soaked bills, and a driver's license, but no credit cards: He does not use them. Marveling at his luck, he set the crumbling bills aside, he said, "as a sort of keepsake." □

#38466711

Herbert Belisle spent part of World War II at a military supply depot on a coral beach in Finschhafen, New Guinea. When the twenty-four-year-old American staff sergeant was posted to this South Pacific base in 1943, he was wearing a pair of copper-nickel alloy dog tags, but he lost them soon after his arrival. The army issued him a new pair, this time made of steel, and he forgot about the first ones.

The lost tags lay in the New Guinea sand for more than four decades, until a vacationing couple from New Zealand happened upon them during a walk along the shore. Later, the visitors turned the tags over to an acquaintance, Greg Henderson, an insurance man in the New Guinea town of Lae. Carrying the serial number 38466711, the tags also bore the name and address of Belisle's next of kin. Hoping to find the tags' original owner, Henderson wrote to the sheriff in Morris, Oklahoma, the hometown listed on the tags, to ask about Belisle.

The former sergeant had not lived in Morris for forty years, but the sheriff tracked Belisle down by contacting his mother and sent Henderson the new address. Henderson wrote to Belisle, describing the discovery. Surprised and pleased by the news that his first dog tags had reappeared after forty-three years, Belisle quickly replied. The next letter from New Zealand had a special enclosure: the missing tags, somewhat blackened by corrosion, but intact and still legible. □

This x-ray image confirmed that Sampson, a Doberman pup, had gulped down an object that even he could not stomach: his master's expensive wristwatch.

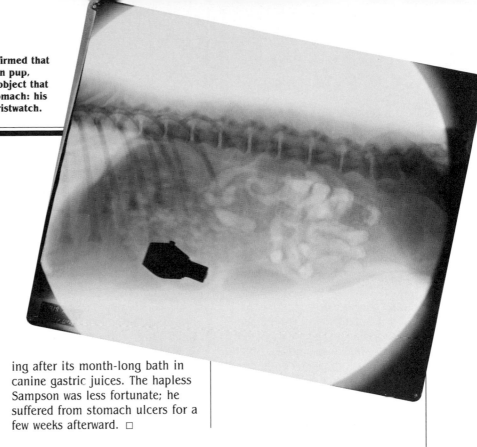

This x-ray image confirmed that Sampson, a Doberman pup, had gulped down an object that even he could not stomach: his master's expensive wristwatch.

Watchdog

In August 1988, a $3,800 silver-and-gold Rolex watch popped off the wrist of Scott Aszkenas and, to his surprise, somehow disappeared in his bedroom. The Spartanburg, South Carolina, news photographer searched in vain for the expensive timepiece, aided, off and on, by Sampson, his five-month-old Doberman pinscher.

About a month later, Aszkenas noticed a lump in the puppy's stomach. On further examination, the bulge turned out to be the missing Rolex. A veterinary surgeon retrieved the watch, which emerged undamaged and still ticking after its month-long bath in canine gastric juices. The hapless Sampson was less fortunate; he suffered from stomach ulcers for a few weeks afterward. □

Leftovers

Almost everything that boards trains and buses along with millions of passengers each day gets off with them. In San Francisco's Bay Area Rapid Transit, or BART, system, only about sixty items a day turn up in the authority's lost-and-found office. The Washington, D.C., Metro logs in some ninety objects daily, while, unaccountably, the much larger New York City Metropolitan Transit Authority averages only about twenty-five.

On the whole, objects lost in transit tend to be the usual things people carry with them, such as wallets, umbrellas, and various personal papers, including income tax returns. There are, however, some perplexing exceptions: false teeth, bicycles, and, a New York official recalls, "an artificial arm, from the elbow down to the five fingers. Twice. The same arm." □

Abandoned and forgotten objects of every description are turned in each day at the lost and found department of the Washington, D.C., transit system.

No Bones

The early human known as Peking Man made a humble debut in 1927 when a team of scientists identified a pair of prehistoric human teeth among some fossils excavated from a cave near the village of Choukoutien, about twenty-five miles from the Chinese capital. Over the next decade, the cave yielded many more bones along with tools and other evidence of early human habitation.

By the outbreak of World War II, the Choukoutien collection had grown to include the bones of forty men, women, and children. Housed and studied at the Peking Union Medical College, the ancient bones were considered a prize of incalculable worth. When hostilities began in Asia, Chinese authorities were eager to keep the scientific treasure from falling into the hands of the advancing Japanese.

In 1941, the Chinese arranged with the American embassy to have the precious fossils spirited out of the country to the United States for safekeeping. Specially crated, the bones of Peking Man went with an escort of nine marines being evacuated on a special train to the port city of Chinwangtao, where the American steamship *President Harrison* awaited them. But the scheme quickly unraveled. The crew of the *President Harrison* grounded their ship rather than let it be captured by the invaders. The marines were returned to Peking as prisoners of the Japanese. And the boxes containing the remains of Peking Man vanished utterly.

The search for them continues. Some researchers believe they were simply lost in the confusion of war, perhaps destroyed or discarded when Japanese troops ransacked the train carrying the marines. Perhaps the bones made it to a Chinwangtao warehouse but fell victim to subsequent bombing or looting. Perhaps traditional Chinese druggists gained possession of the fossils and ground them up for sale as the healing compound known as dragon bones *(page 90)*. Despite claims and counterclaims about the present location of the fossils, most observers believe that Peking Man's remains are gone forever, leaving only drawings and plaster casts to mark his place in human evolution. □

Fragile Folios

Of the 14 million books shelved in the U.S. Library of Congress, 3.5 million are too fragile to handle: The simple act of turning their pages would cause their brittle paper to crumble away. And each year, an estimated 77,000 more volumes in the national collection join the ranks of the disastrously frail, unable to survive the touch of a reader's hand. It is a problem faced by libraries everywhere. Books are self-destructing, being eaten away by corrosive chemicals in their paper, and taking with them the recent intellectual record of the human race.

Older knowledge has a kind of immunity, however. Books printed before the mid-nineteenth century endure far longer than modern publications. For example, many books from the sixteenth century are still in excellent condition today, while most of those printed in the last hundred fifty years have a life expectancy reckoned in decades.

The difference lies with a technological change in the way paper is manufactured. In the nineteenth century, acidic chemicals were introduced to the process of papermaking, creating paper that is ultimately destroyed by the latent acids it contains. Books printed on such paper have a shelf life of only about fifty years.

Although such preservation techniques as microfilming and treating books with deacidifying chemicals can arrest the process of self-destruction, it is slow, expensive work. Preserving only the American Library of Congress collection by these means would take an estimated $100 million and twenty years. In the meantime, custodians of the world's books hope that publishers will return to the long-lived, acid-free paper on which earlier knowledge has been preserved, it seems, forever. □

The potent chemistry between Greta Garbo and costar Lars Harmon could not save *Divine Woman*, which, like hundreds of contemporary movies, fell victim to the volatile chemistry of nitrate-based film.

Fading Stars

"These our actors, as I foretold you, were all spirits and are melted into air, into thin air." Prospero's famous stage farewell in Shakespeare's *Tempest* aptly describes the unhappy fate of another brand of famous actors. Film supposedly confers a certain immortality on its stars, whose performances can be played over and over again, as a stage actor's cannot. In fact, what was thought to be a permanent record of great work has turned out to be sadly ephemeral.

Of more than 21,000 feature films produced in the United States from the 1890s through 1950, as many as half survive only in memory. The American Film Institute estimates that only 15 percent of the films of the 1920s still exist today; the survival rate for those of earlier decades is even lower. Among the missing are such classics as *The Divine Woman* with Greta Garbo, *That Royle Girl* with W. C. Fields, *The Rogue Song* with Laurel and Hardy, *The Young Rajah* with Rudolph Valentino, and the silent 1919 *Cleopatra*, starring Theda Bara as the sultry Egyptian queen. Performances by stars as

diverse as John Barrymore, Lillian Gish, Lon Chaney, and Gloria Swanson have disappeared, along with work of such revered directors as Frank Capra, D. W. Griffith, Ernst Lubitsch, Josef von Sternberg, and Eric von Stroheim.

Some of these vanished films were lost, discarded, or destroyed by the industry that produced them. Many films, however, were victims of simple chemistry, self-destructing as the plastic on which they were printed either burst into flames or decayed into gelatinous goo and dry powder. Cellulose nitrate, the plastic of choice for American feature films until 1951, is a highly flammable and chemi-

cally unstable compound. It ignites at a lower temperature than wood, burns far more rapidly, and blazes on even when doused with water and extinguishing foam. Moreover, as nitrate ages, it gives off gases that combine with moisture in the air to produce acids that eat away at the film.

Climate-controlled storage can slow the deterioration process, and old movies can be transposed from celluloid to a more durable plastic, but these preservation techniques are slow and expensive. As archives race to save the cinematic past from extinction, more and more irreplaceable performances are melting into thin air. □

Disappearing Days

In 46 BC, the Roman emperor Julius Caesar abolished the use of calendars based on the phases of the moon and adopted a sun-based system. This so-called Julian calendar supposed the year to consist of 365 and a quarter days—just 11 minutes and 14 seconds longer than the actual solar year, during which the earth makes a complete circuit around the sun. Although it worked reasonably well for a ◊

In this 1582 painting, Pope Gregory XIII *(far left)* presides over astronomers who calculated his new calendar.

time, the inexorable loss of one day every 128 years gradually caused the calendar to drift out of phase with the seasons.

Thus, when Pope Gregory XIII promulgated his carefully calculated reform calendar in 1582, he had to accommodate a difference of 10 days. He did so by making them disappear: The day after October 4 simply became October 15. Much of Christian Europe quickly adopted the pope's new calendar, which embraced a year that was 365 days, 5 hours, 49 minutes, and 12 seconds long.

By the time England switched to the Gregorian system in 1752, the old Julian deficit had grown to 11 days. September 3 was therefore transformed by decree into September 14, causing workers to riot over the matter of lost pay.

Japan adopted the Gregorian calendar in 1873, losing a full dozen days in the process. In 1918, Russia's revolutionary government set the Soviet calendar to the Gregorian standard by making the first of February the 14th. (As a result of this contraction, the Soviets celebrate their October Revolution in November.) China shifted to the Gregorian calendar in 1949.

Still, this widely used calendrical system is not perfect. To keep the calendar in step with the sun, every year divisible by four is designated a leap year, in which a twenty-ninth day is added to February; the exceptions are the opening years of centuries, which are leap years only if divisible by 400; the year 2000 will have an extra day, but the year 3000 will not. Despite such corrections, the Gregorian year remains 26 seconds longer than the true solar year calculated by astronomers. □

Marking Time

A nagging human urge to speak to the future has created the time capsule, a container of contemporary artifacts buried away for the eyes of generations to come. They are like notes in bottles, tossed into the river of time; like most such communiqués, many vanish en route. For every time capsule that completes its journey through time, several thousand are forgotten, according to University of Arizona sociologist Albert Bergesen and his archaeologist colleague William Rathje.

Cases in point abound. When New York's Pulitzer Building was torn down in 1956, workers found a sealed copper box. It had been buried in one of the cornerstones in 1889 and contained coins, photographs, and commemorative medallions, along with what may have been the only surviving set of blueprints showing its location. It was recovered purely by accident.

When Wilkinsburg, Pennsylvania, celebrated its hundredth anniversary in 1987, residents decided to open a time capsule buried there twenty-five years earlier. But no one knew where the capsule had been placed. Apparently, members of the capsule committee had refused to divulge its location at the time, and as years passed and committee members died, the secret was lost as well.

In 1959, officials in Olympia, Washington, had to use a metal detector to find a one-ton capsule buried for the state's territorial centennial only six years before. Since then, a marker has been put in place, but according to Kirkland, Washington, writer Knute Berger, not in the right spot.

Berger was hired by the state to design a capsule that would not disappear before its time. His seven-foot-tall steel container, which marks the hundredth year of statehood, sits in plain sight in the capitol, served by more than three hundred young keepers of the capsule. They have volunteered to keep it intact and to recruit another group of youngsters in twenty-five years. Thus, knowledge of the capsule's whereabouts, and its contents, will pass from generation to generation.

But even certain knowledge of a capsule's location is sometimes not enough to make the enclosed message accessible. For example, a small metal cylinder containing memorabilia for the future is buried snugly beneath the eighteen-ton magnet of an atom smasher on the campus of the Massachusetts Institute of Technology.

The term *time capsule* was coined for the New York World's Fair in 1939. What was then the Westinghouse Electric and Manufacturing Company buried a torpedo-size, copper-alloy container at the fair site in Flushing Meadows, to be opened in the year 6939. Its location and contents were detailed in a book sent to libraries around the world. But today, some fifty years later, copies are rare; the book has apparently vanished even from the U.S. Library of Congress. Westinghouse itself has only one copy but hopes to preserve it for the forty-nine and a half centuries still to go. □

THE VANISH

A glittering gold coin, clipped between a pair of outstretched fingertips, suddenly flickers and is gone. An elephant, standing at the center of a brightly lighted stage, abruptly vanishes from view. A frightening apparition, hovering above the heads of an enthralled theater audience, slowly fades into nothingness.

In the world of magic, such illusions, or effects, are called vanishes, and one does not make something disappear—one "vanishes" it. Nothing else in the magician's bag of tricks compares; the sight of something or someone being inexplicably transported into oblivion sends a shudder of wonderment and horror, fascination and fear through the human spirit. From the earliest days of magic, the vanish has reigned as king of illusions.

In some of its modern incarnations, however, the vanishing effect occurs on an even larger stage: Whole armies disappear into the confusion of camouflage, and squadrons of aircraft attack invisibly, cloaked by a technological vanish called Stealth.

3

First Sleight

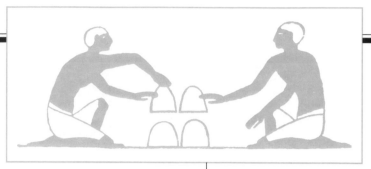

Writing in the third century AD, Athenian social commentator and rhetorician Alciphron described a demonstration of skill that left him "almost speechless" with surprise. "A man came forward," he reported, "and placed on a three-legged table three small dishes, under which he concealed some little white round pebbles. These he placed one by one under the dishes, and then, I do not know how, made them appear altogether under one. At other times he made them disappear from beneath the dishes, and showed them in his mouth." Alciphron observed several more feats, until at last the conjurer caused the stones "to vanish from the sight of everyone."

After puzzling over the performance, Alciphron admitted he could not penetrate the

man's secret. In fact, the scribe found the manipulations so devious that he would have been loath to invite the conjurer into his home. "He would steal everything I had," concluded Alciphron, "and strip my farm of all it contains."

This clever manipulation of reality was already ancient when Alciphron saw it. He was one of many thousands of people who, over the centuries, have been baffled by the sleight-of-hand trick known as the cups and balls. The feat, in which three balls are made to

vanish, reappear, and vanish again beneath three cups, is surely the oldest magic trick in the world, perhaps dating as far back as 2200 BC. Some historians believe that a 4,190-year-old hieroglyphic discovered on the walls of an Egyptian tomb at Beni Hasan shows two figures conjuring with cups and balls *(above)*. The trick remains a popular staple for most professional magicians, even though its secret (a concealed, fourth ball) is revealed in nearly every child's magic set. And it even has a royal following. In 1978, the prince of Wales was awarded a membership in the Magic Circle, Great Britain's exclusive conjurer's society, on the condition that he perform a sleight-of-hand effect. His selection: the cups and balls. □

In this painting by fifteenth-century Dutch artist Hieronymus Bosch, a conjurer astounds his audience with a rendition of the cups and balls, as an onlooker's purse gets picked.

Blackstone's Ducks

Because most vanishes take place in plain sight, the real trick is getting the audience to look somewhere else when the effect happens, using what magicians call misdirection. A fundamental technique of any illusion, misdirection leads the observer's eye toward some decoy action for the fraction of a second it takes to accomplish the disappearance.

No one used misdirection to better effect than the great Harry Blackstone, a modern American magician noted for his spectacular vanishes. Among magicians, in fact, the classic tale of misdirection is that of Blackstone's so-called duck vanish *(above)*. The magician would lead a parade of quacking ducks into a small enclosure at the center of the stage and announce that he would shortly cause them to disappear. Then, as he prepared to vanish them, the suspenseful moment was shattered by an assistant, entering from the wings, who tripped and fell heavily to the stage. Blackstone would glare at the clumsy aide for a time, then compose himself and return to the ducks. When the enclosure was opened, the birds had indeed disappeared.

Night after night, the awkward assistant stumbled at the same spot on stage, at the same moment in Blackstone's act. Night after night, Blackstone turned and glared, drawing every eye in the theater toward the interruption. And night after night, at that precise moment, another, quieter helper secretly marched the well-trained ducks offstage. □

The Old Vanishing Coin Trick

Misdirection, the time-honored magician's art of temporarily diverting the audience's attention, can make large magic from a small effect. Indeed, a small-scale trick performed at close range can be as mystifying as a disappearing elephant. The sleight-of-hand trick illustrated here, performed with only a napkin, a salt shaker, and a coin, demonstrates the power of magic that takes place, in the old circus master's phrase, "right before your very eyes."

1
The magician begins by showing a coin and announcing that he will cause it to vanish.

2
After placing the coin on the table, he picks up an ordinary salt shaker and "stamps" the coin with it, as if pounding it into the table.

6
With his right hand, the magician bangs the salt shaker onto the coin once more.

7
The coin, however, fails to vanish.

8
Frustrated, the magician flicks the coin a few inches forward with his left index finger. Then he pauses, as if suddenly remembering.

xt, he wraps the salt shaker in a
oth or paper napkin.

4
Holding the wrapped salt shaker by
the neck, the magician repeats the
stamping motion.

5
The magician pauses to show the
coin—and the salt shaker inside
the napkin—one last time. "With a
snap of my fingers," he declares,
"the coin will vanish!"

ait!" he says. "It wasn't the *coin*
at was supposed to vanish . . ."
e right hand sets down what ap-
ars to be the wrapped salt shak-
and, with a sharp rap, the left
nd flattens the empty napkin.

10
"It was the salt shaker!"

THE SECRET: Because
the magician does not say
that the salt shaker will
vanish, the audience fo-
cuses on the coin, espe-
cially when the trick ap-
pears to fail. He flicks the
coin, providing the crucial
misdirection, while his
right hand (holding the
shaker) swings back to the
edge of the table, letting
the shaker fall silently out
of the napkin into his lap.
If he leans forward slightly
to flick the coin, his right
arm swings back naturally
to rest on his right elbow.
This movement covers the
salt shaker drop. No one
is suspicious, because the
napkin retains the shaker's
shape (paper napkins are
best, but cloth will do).
Onlookers assume the salt
shaker is still inside the
napkin—until the magi-
cian springs the surprise.

An Elusive Illusion

The famed Indian rope trick, which involves a coil of rope extended skyward, is a visual synonym for all oriental magic. But the secret of this fabled vanish has eluded conjurers and scholars for centuries. Indeed, some magicians believe the trick is simply a myth, and they dismiss eyewitness reports as the products of mass hypnosis or some form of shared vision. Still, a few conjurers cling to the hope that the trick is real and, once its secret is known, reproducible.

A remarkable early account by an Arab traveler tells of a fourteenth-century Chinese magician who presented the effect in the open courtyard of the khan's palace in Hangchau. The conjurer began his demonstration by displaying a long coil of leather fastened to a wooden ball. As the palace guests watched, he hurled the ball into the air. Instead of returning to earth, the ball soared higher and higher and finally seemed to disappear into low-lying clouds, leaving the long strip of leather dangling behind. A small boy in the magician's troupe grabbed the leather rope and began to climb up hand over hand until he, too, was swallowed by clouds. The magician called for the boy to return, but no answer came. Growing angry, he called out again, but still there was no reply. Finally, the man could no longer contain his wrath. Armed with a razor-edged scimitar, he followed the boy up the rope and into the low-hanging clouds. A moment later, the crowd heard screams of pain, and a small object fell from the sky into the courtyard, with a horrifying plop. The curious visi-tors gathered around it, then recoiled in horror—the object was a boy's hand. An instant later, another hand thud-ded to earth, followed by a foot, a head, a torso, an-other foot, and, finally, a bloody jumble of innards.

Apparently satisfied that justice had been done, the ma-gician reappeared, sliding down the rope. Then, very carefully, he began fitting the tangled heap of body parts into a crude human shape. When he finished, he gave the form a sharp kick. The boy—now miraculously whole and re-stored to life—jumped to his feet, apparently having learned a painful lesson.

In the audience, the Arab travel-er found himself so overcome by the ghastly spectacle that he fell to the ground, suffering from heart palpitations. When he revived, the other guests chided him for his reaction. The miracle he had wit-nessed, they assured him, had been a mere conjurer's trick.

Many of the world's greatest ma-gicians have traveled to India in the hope of tracing the origin of the effect but to no avail. And attempts to reproduce it onstage have fallen considerably short of the original. For a time it seemed that the trick was destined to re-main eternally out of reach.

In 1955, however, an Indian gu-ru named Sadhu Vadramakrishna came forward, claiming that long ago he had performed the effect himself. Although his account was

Performing in England in 1934, Karachi and his son Kyder boggled minds by staging their version of the Indian rope trick in broad daylight.

somewhat vague (and did not explain reports of daytime shows), Vadramakrishna revealed that the Indian rope trick, when executed at night, owed much of its success to bright torches that partially blinded the spectators, prohibiting them from seeing more than about ten feet into the darkened sky.

By way of preparation, the magician would stretch a thin wire between the highest branches of two tall trees. The rope that he hurled skyward at the start of the performance was fitted with a stout hook that grappled the wire and held the rope suspended in air. According to Vadramakrishna, both he and his assistant—like all such performers—were skilled acrobats who could easily climb to the top of the rope and remain perched on the high wire. To spectators peering through the glare of the torches, it looked as if both had been swallowed by the night.

The Indian magician even had a means of re-creating the gruesome midair dismemberment of legend. While balanced on the wire, he simply threw down pieces of dead monkey that he had concealed in his cloak. Later, when he slipped back down the rope, he hid his assistant in the cloak's billowing folds, in preparation for producing him in his "restored" state.

Other enticing testimony to the rope trick's reality came in 1985, when British magician Paul Daniels experienced a curious coincidence while preparing an elaborate outdoor staging of the Indian rope trick for a television special. To lend authentic atmosphere to his performance, Daniels had engaged an Indian orchestra to provide background music. As he discussed the musical selections with the orchestra's conductor, Daniels mentioned that he would be performing the famous Indian rope

trick. "Oh," said the musician blandly, "I've seen that." Questioned further, he recalled seeing a group of traveling performers stage the effect during his boyhood, in the district of Rajasthan.

Soon afterward, Daniels suffered a serious burn while practicing a fire trick. The injury did not interfere with his television work, but the magician promised his doctors that he would have the dressing changed regularly. The following week, after a long day of filming in Inverness, Scotland, Daniels went to a local hospital to have his bandages changed. In the course of the treatment, Daniels told his physician, a Dr. Singh, about his attempt to re-create the Indian rope trick. Without missing a beat, the doctor replied, "Oh, I've seen that." Thunderstruck, Daniels listened as the Indian physician recalled that he had seen the trick as a boy—in Rajasthan. □

Smoke and Mirrors

Magicians guard their secrets with an almost fanatical jealousy, and many swear their assistants to a lifetime of silence. Such secrecy not only protects the performer's livelihood but also preserves a mystery that is essential to both magicians and their audiences. As the first-century Roman philosopher Seneca put it, "Show me how the trick is done, and I have lost my interest therein." Nothing vanishes a good effect faster than exposure. The so-called ghost shows that once held European audiences spellbound are a case in point, for

they endured only for as long as they amazed—then disappeared from the repertoire of magic.

The ghost-show sensation began in the turbulent years that followed the French Revolution, when an enterprising magician named Étienne-Gaspard Robertson first staged his eerie "Phantasmagoria." In an abandoned, candlelit chapel near the Place Vendôme in Paris, Robertson caused realistic ghosts and phantoms to appear for frightened crowds of ticket-holders.

He opened each performance by explaining, in appropriately hushed

tones, that he would shortly produce manifestations of the dead— not a sight for the faint of heart. Then, as the candles in the chapel were slowly extinguished, Robertson poured blood, vitriol, and other acids into a brazier containing white hot coals. As a sizzling column of smoke billowed upward, sinister goblins and leering phantoms danced in the guttering light of the coals. Some of the apparitions were well known to the French audiences: The famous writer Voltaire appeared nightly, as did the revolutionaries Marat and Robespierre, and the philosopher Rousseau. Other specters were ◊

less distinguished but no less fearsome. One man, convinced that he had seen the ghost of his late wife, fled the chapel.

In the finale, Death itself appeared from the shadows in the form of a skeleton bearing a glistening scythe. The creature grew larger and ever more menacing as it advanced toward the audience. Few were unmoved, as Death's ominous footfalls echoed through the chapel. Many fainted and had to be carried from the scene.

In reality, Robertson's ghostly displays had nothing to do with the supernatural. He achieved his terrifying effects through the clever manipulation of a device then called a magic lantern, an early version of today's slide projector. His ghosts and phantoms were nothing more than figures painted on glass slides and ingeniously projected directly onto the columns of smoke that rose from his hot coals and made the images seem to move. By rolling the lantern forward and back on a track, the apparitions could be made to move and grow larger. With elaborate double slides, Robertson could even cause a figure's mouth and eyes to move. When the magic lantern was extinguished, the phantoms vanished as mysteriously as they had appeared. It represented an enormous leap in the technology of magic.

In 1862, British chemist John Pepper adapted the techniques of the Phantasmagoria to throw an even greater scare into the people of England. As director of London's Polytechnic Institute, a kind of showplace for the unusual, he gained renown for his instructive scientific demonstrations. Occa-

In the 1860s, the effect called Pepper's Ghost amazed British audiences by using a projected image of a specter to spin the illusion of a ghostly actor joining the real one on stage.

sionally, he lectured before Queen Victoria herself. So mindful was he of the honor that he grandly announced one experiment by saying, "The oxygen and the hydrogen will now have the honor of combining before your Majesty."

Scientific pretensions aside, Pepper was a master showman. His scholarly style of lecturing made his performances seem all the more real. So, too, did the new technique that he employed, in which a bright light and a heavy sheet of glass angled so as to be invisible to the audience were used to produce an illusion of spirits. The light illuminated a figure concealed offstage so that its reflection seemed to hover above the stage. Known as Pepper's Ghost, the effect could create remarkable tableaux. Ghostly images shared the stage with flesh-and-blood ac-

tors. Sometimes a swashbuckling star would engage in a life-or-death duel with a phantom, finally skewering the apparition on the point of his sword. Such scenes had to be carefully blocked and choreographed, because the players onstage could not see the images reflected on the glass.

Permutations of Pepper's Ghost were quickly developed. In Vienna a startling display, known as the Room of Mortality, began as the curtains parted to show a room painted entirely blue. An audience member was escorted from his seat and shown into an upright coffin that stood at the rear of the stage. Offstage, assistants swung an invisible slab of glass into position over the coffin and turned the lantern on an accomplice dressed as a skeleton. To the audience, the effect was nightmarish—the reflect-

ed skeleton was superimposed on the volunteer, who seemed to wither into nothingness, leaving only bones in his place. A moment later, the lantern went out, the reflected skeleton vanished, and the victim returned to his seat, none the worse for the experience.

In a sense, curiosity killed the ghost shows. At one Austrian performance, a skeptical spectator used a slingshot to fire a stone at the ghostly presence. The projectile smashed against the heavy glass sheet, which cracked and then shattered, raining hundreds of pounds of jagged glass upon the stage. In time, the once-remarkable secret became so widely known that even children in the audiences were no longer fooled; they delighted in hurling paper wads at the stage to see them bounce off the glass sheet. □

Only a Bird in a Vanished Cage

"An iron cage with a canary inside, held high in the air, suddenly disappears, without even the melodramatic lightning flash, which, according to all tradition, should accompany such a mysterious flight." So a London newspaper lauded the 1873 debut of a new effect (composed of about equal parts classic misdirection and painstaking mechanical preparation) created by the innovative French conjurer Buatier de Kolta. Known as the Flying Birdcage, it held audiences spellbound from its first performance.

But the effect also raised the issue of whether the vanishing bird

was harmed during the magician's act. While touring London in 1921, American showman Carl Hertz suddenly found himself asked that question by a group of officials from the Royal Society for the Prevention of Cruelty to Animals. A performing-animals bill, designed to protect creatures used in stage productions, was then under consideration in Parliament. Hertz, who caused a canary to disappear several times each day, ranked high on the list of suspected offenders. His accusers feared that the birds used in his performances were often maimed and possibly even killed as the birdcage was

whisked away to parts unknown.

An indignant Hertz immediately took the offensive. Only the worst kind of bungler would allow any harm to come to his canaries, the magician insisted. His own feathered assistants, said Hertz, had remained in his safe care for years, none the worse for their rigorous performing schedule. The American's protests only added fuel to the controversy, and Hertz soon found himself forced to appear before a Select Committee of Britain's House of Commons. One of Hertz's accusers, a theater manager by the name of Haverley, offered to pay the showman a hundred ◊

pounds if he could prove that the bird suffered no injury. For his own part, Hertz volunteered to make a large donation to charity if he could not vanish a bird and then have it reappear unharmed.

Far more than a hundred pounds was at stake when Hertz presented himself at the House of Commons on August 2, 1921. If he were found guilty of cruelty to animals, his career would suffer irreparable damage. Without question, this performance before a small group of British lawmakers was to be the most important of his career.

Hertz appeared confident as he addressed his stern-faced jury. Dressed in full stage costume, the performer offered the committee members a close look at the bird-cage grasped firmly between his outstretched hands. He then pre-sented Connie, a favorite among his flock of canaries, and invited the committee to tag the bird to avoid any possibility of substitu-tion or other deception. Connie then took her place in the bird-cage, apparently unconcerned by the drama unfolding around her.

Without warning, Hertz gave a loud cry and threw both hands over his head—and in that instant the cage vanished without a trace. The feat so startled one of the commit-tee members that he jumped up from his seat. Hertz, meanwhile, quickly peeled off his suitcoat and

Charged with cruelty to animals, magician Carl Hertz had to prove that his famous vanishing birdcage feat did not harm the star, a canary named Connie.

excused himself from the officials' chamber, returning a moment later with the unharmed Connie perched upon his finger. "I do not want Mr. Haverley's hundred pounds," he said when the committee had agreed to drop its charges of ani-mal cruelty. "I am glad to do the trick for nothing."

Actually, the episode was worth far more to Hertz in

the free publicity it generated, for his career had been somewhat on the wane. With the renewed burst of popularity that followed their performance in the House of Com-mons, he and his vanishing birds continued to tour with the Flying Birdcage for the rest of his life. □

Gone!

Each year, thousands of magicians' assistants vanish from the stages of the world, leaving little more than a puff of smoke in their wake. The first of them disappeared from view in Paris on April 27, 1886, the evening chosen by French magician Buatier de Kolta to introduce a stunning new illusion at the Eden Theatre.

A complex optical trick requiring elaborate stage preparation and split-second timing, the effect began simply enough as de Kolta entered from the wings with a large piece of newspaper tucked under his arm. Explaining that he did not want anyone to think he had stooped to the use of a trapdoor, he spread the paper flat on the stage. Next, the conjurer positioned a fragile-looking wooden chair at the center of the newspaper and instructed his assistant to sit down facing the audience. As soon as she settled herself, de Kolta covered her with a large silk cloth.

With a sharp flick of his wrist, de Kolta snatched the silk away, then turned to bask in the thunderous applause of his audience. The lady had disappeared, instantly, as if swallowed up by the silk covering. As an added flourish, de Kolta flicked the silk above his head. The cloth, too, vanished from his hands.

The Vanishing Lady became de Kolta's masterpiece, a jewel in the crown of the most influential magician of the day. As news of the master's new effect spread, women began disappearing from stages all across the globe. Within a few years, however, the illusion had

become so common that its popularity declined. Magicians began searching for new and better ways of making their assistants vanish. Many variations of the de Kolta illusion surfaced, but only one—devised by the Belgian magician Servais Le Roy—could be said to match the original's impact.

Le Roy introduced his magnificent new vanish at the Empire Theater in Johannesburg in 1905. Beckoning his wife, Talma, onto the stage, he waved his fingers before her face, apparently causing her to fall into a trance. He carefully placed her on a narrow platform and covered her with a sheet of thin cloth. Slowly passing his hands over the platform, Le Roy produced the first of two apparent miracles. While all eyes remained fixed upon the form of Talma, still clearly visible beneath the thin covering, she gently floated up and drifted out over the audience.

After a moment, Le Roy gestured toward her from the stage, and the floating figure began a slow descent. The trick appeared to be ending as Talma hovered near the platform, but the magician had an even greater surprise in store. As the covered form moved within reach, Le Roy grasped a corner of the cloth and whisked it away—revealing only empty space. The floating lady had vanished.

Like Le Roy, the British team of John Maskelyne and David Devant proved unusually adept at improving and updating familiar effects. Over the years, the pair vanished hundreds of ladies from the stage of their famed Egyptian Hall in London, although they seldom did it the same way for more than one season. One of their greatest feats, first performed in August 1905, was the Mascot Moth, which many magicians still consider the finest vanishing lady effect ever devised.

Devant claimed that the idea came to him one night while he slept. In a dream, the magician saw a demonic figure tempting a helpless moth toward the flame ⟳

of a candle. As the creature fluttered near the fire, it disappeared abruptly, as if closing up on itself. Devant locked himself away in his workshop and emerged some time later with a plan for bringing his dream to life onstage.

At the start of the illusion, a "moth-woman," dressed in a flowing white dress with wings attached, danced across the darkened stage. Devant, in full evening dress, approached her, bearing a lighted candle. As the magician drew near, the woman folded her wings in front of her, as if to protect herself from the flame. In the twinkling of an eye, the wings collapsed upon themselves and vanished—and she was gone. The effect was one of the most striking Devant had ever presented. After each presentation, as an added touch, he would turn to his mystified audience and announce wryly, "I leave the stage for a few moments after each experiment in order to give you an opportunity to tell each other how it is done." But Devant kept the secret of the Mascot Moth.

One of Devant's admirers, the American Harry Blackstone, also had a gift for finding miracles in unlikely places—and for devising effects no one else could plumb. Blackstone's close friend and adviser was the famed author Walter Gibson, creator of Lamont Cranston, also known as the Shadow, all-knowing scourge of the underworld. Blackstone frequently relaxed backstage with a Gibson novel. One afternoon in 1936, he found himself particularly enthralled. In the story, the Shadow, while being chased by thugs, raced across an auto junkyard and dived into a stack of old tires. When his pursuers fell on the tires and tossed them aside, the wily crime-fighter had disappeared.

As he closed the book, Blackstone knew he would have to duplicate the amazing feat onstage. In short order, he was presenting the puzzling Auto Tire Mystery, in which an assistant disappeared after being ringed from head to toe with a stack of brightly colored tires. How did Blackstone do it? Not even the Shadow knows. □

The Missing Elephant

"Make it big" was the motto of a magician who billed himself as the Great Lafayette *(page 73)*, but it was Harry Houdini, one of history's great showmen, who best applied the adage to a vanish. Noting that other magicians of his day were drawing crowds by causing donkeys and horses to disappear, Houdini reasoned that a larger subject might attract a larger audience. Accordingly, he set his sights on the biggest land animal of all: He would vanish an elephant.

Houdini's theater program breathlessly described the effect. "Before one's very eyes," it read, "in a full blaze of light, with bewildering rapidity, this pachyderm monster suddenly eludes the vision." The monster, actually a friendly creature named Jennie, first took the stage with Houdini on January 7, 1918. The elephant immediately won over the audience by rearing up on her back legs and bowing politely to the crowd—neatly upstaging the Great Houdini. Meanwhile, a team of assistants wheeled an eight-foot-square cabinet onto the stage. It had curtains at the front and hinged doors at the back, while the floor, sides, and top were solid planking. A rolling platform twenty-six inches high enabled spectators to see beneath the cabinet, prohibiting the use of a trapdoor.

While Houdini said a few words to the audience, Jennie gave a smart salute with her trunk, climbed a short ramp, and was led into the cabinet by her trainer. The curtains were then closed over the front of the box to shield the creature from view. An instant later, Houdini fired a pistol. Then his assistants flung open the curtains—the elephant was gone. To complete the effect, Houdini opened the rear doors of the cabinet, affording a clear view to the rear wall of the stage. The elephant had simply vanished and would do so twice a day for the next nineteen weeks. In the excitement, only a handful of spectators noticed that the elephant's trainer had also disappeared.

The spectacle became a sensation and resulted in the longest single theater booking of Houdini's career. "I have been prolonged at the Hippodrome as the vanishing elephant is creating so much talk," Houdini boasted in a letter to friends, "and really it is the biggest vanish the world has ever seen." Indeed, it was so big that it could be performed only on the giant stage of the Hippodrome.

Few magic effects have generated more debate. Jealous rivals, pointing out that only six stagehands rolled the cabinet onto the stage, while twenty were needed to roll it off, claimed that Jennie had been concealed inside the box. But few really believed that Houdini, whose daring escapes required extraordinary planning and attention to detail, would have been so obvious. Other magicians suggested that, despite the fact that the cabinet was raised, Jennie had managed to slip out through a trapdoor. However, in order to do so, the elephant would have needed an oxygen tank. Beneath the stage was a pool containing 250,000 gallons of water, used in the theater's popular water spectacles.

To this day magicians remain divided as to how the trick was accomplished. And Houdini himself provided no clues. When asked for the secret behind his most famous vanish, the magician would invariably reply, "Even the elephant doesn't know how it is done." □

Houdini's elephant, Jennie, greets the magician before he vanishes her in front of a Hippodrome audience.

Basket of Death

While traveling through India in the 1870s, an English clergyman looked on in horror as a Hindu conjurer forced a young girl into a squat, loosely woven wicker basket, then savagely pierced the basket again and again with a sword. But when the magician at last held up the basket to the audience, it was empty. Moments later, the vanished girl reappeared, unharmed.

This classic illusion remains a staple of stage and street magicians to this day. One of the dazzling variations on the theme is shown at right, as the Pendragons, Jonathan and Charlotte, put their modern stamp upon the venerable East Indian Basket Mystery.

1
With a flourish, Charlotte slips into a large wicker basket . . .

2
. . . and, obscured briefly by a split-second snap of Jonathan's cape, disappears from view.

5
A moment later, Charlotte's hand rises gracefully from the deadly steel crossfire.

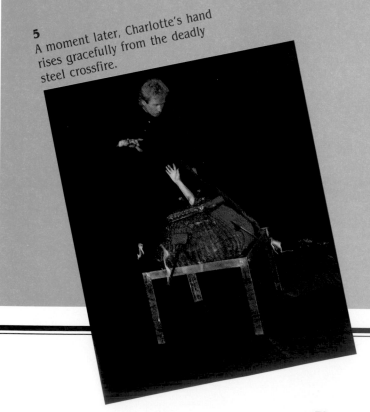

6
Now the *coup de grâce:* a broadsword thrust straight down through the center of the basket, certain death for any occupant.

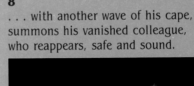

4
. . . Jonathan drives four flaming swords (a unique Pendragon touch) through the container's flanks.

3
After verifying that his partner is indeed inside the basket . . .

8
. . . with another wave of his cape, summons his vanished colleague, who reappears, safe and sound.

7
But . . . Charlotte is gone. Jonathan steps into the basket to prove it is empty, then . . .

The Vanish of a Lifetime

Magicians often disappear. But one little-known conjurer named William Ellsworth Robinson failed to reappear; when Robinson vanished, he vanished for good.

Born in New York City in 1861, Robinson gained modest recognition by designing magical effects for such famous performers as Harry Kellar and Herrmann the Great. As a stage magician, however, he achieved only slight success. More lucrative bookings went to a group of Chinese magicians headed by an elegant mystifier named Ching Ling Foo, who enjoyed enormous popularity at the turn of the century.

A savvy vaudeville agent, hoping to cash in on Ching Ling Foo's popularity, offered the thirty-nine-year-old Robinson a month's contract at the Folies-Bergère in Paris if he could re-create the Chinese magician's act. Robinson promptly shaved his head and mustache and boarded a ship for France. With the use of make-up, Mandarin silk robes, and a long fake pigtail, the American-born Robinson made a convincing debut in 1900 as a self-styled Marvelous Chinese Conjurer.

Adopting the name of Chung Ling Soo, meaning "very good luck," William Robinson became an immediate sensation. Indeed, his success so eclipsed his previous achievements that he never again appeared as William Robinson. For the next eighteen years, Robinson maintained the persona of Chung Ling Soo onstage and off, even employing an interpreter for interviews with the press. William Robinson had effectively vanished from the face of the earth.

Ching Ling Foo, the man Robinson had so closely imitated, grew understandably incensed by the deception, but a "magic showdown" between the two men was abandoned when Ching Ling Foo failed to appear. By this time, the skill and craft of the impostor had in many ways overtaken the original. To complete the illusion, Robinson's wife, the former Olive Path, adopted the identity of Suee Seen.

Chung Ling Soo carefully maintained his charade. He never spoke onstage except through his interpreter, and many of his illusions were tailored to his adopted heritage. The most famous of these was his Death-Defying Bullet-Catch, in which marksmen fired a pair of muzzleloading guns at the magician, who seemed calmly to pluck the bullets from the air in midflight. The effect, which he

Asked to impersonate a Chinese conjurer, William Ellsworth Robinson vanished into his created persona, Chung Ling Soo, who became the master magician advertised in vibrant posters.

presented as a depiction of his escape from execution during China's Boxer Rebellion, brought Chung Ling Soo even greater fame.

Unfortunately, the effect also brought his new life to a premature end. On March 23, 1918, Chung Ling Soo performed the famous Bullet-Catch for the last time at a London theater. On that evening, when the marksmen fired their rounds, Chung Ling Soo staggered backward and collapsed, clutching his chest. As his wife rushed to his side, the magician spoke his first English words from the stage in over a decade: "My God," he gasped, "I've been shot. Lower the curtain." He died in his wife's arms a short time later.

Many wild rumors surfaced about the performer's dramatic death. Some suggested that Soo, struggling beneath a mountain of debt, had staged a spectacular suicide. Others insisted that he had been murdered, perhaps by jealous rivals. But a coroner's inquest ruled the matter a case of "death by misadventure" after a gunsmith testified that the weapon that had fired the fatal shot had become badly worn over the years. A false chamber, intended to retain the bullet and protect the magician from harm, had instead released the fatal round.

In the end, Chung Ling Soo's greatest illusion—the vanishing of William Robinson—had failed as well. For although his Chinese act fooled the public, his dual identity was an open secret in the magic community. Still, it was such an audacious vanish, his peers would remember him in death only as Chung Ling Soo, the Marvelous Chinese Conjurer. □

Body Double

The Great Lafayette dazzled audiences around the globe during his lifetime, but his most unusual disappearance occurred after his death. A highly original illusionist, Lafayette gained additional renown at the close of the nineteenth century as a quick-change artist, a sharpshooter, and an impressionist. Many of his stage effects featured trained animals, and the performer became well known for his abiding love of the creatures.

His clear favorite was Beauty, a mongrel given him by escape artist Harry Houdini. Beauty, who Lafayette claimed was not a mutt but a "gheckhund" from the Azores, enjoyed a life of uncommon luxury at her master's side. She and he had adjoining bedroom suites in Lafayette's London townhouse; Beauty's featured a miniature sofa and a porcelain bathtub. Visitors to the magician's home were often dismayed to find the dog seated regally at the dinner table, enjoying a full-course meal in advance of the human guests. She also had her own compartment in Lafayette's private railroad car, and her likeness adorned the magician's checks. Lest anyone harbor any doubts about the magician's feeling for his dog, a plaque on the wall of his home spelled it out. "The more I see of men," it read, "the more I love my dog."

Such personal eccentricities fueled the public's interest in Lafayette's performances, and the magician seldom disappointed. His flamboyant act climaxed with a twenty-five-minute spectacle called the Lion's Bride, which showcased the magician's dramatic skill as well as his illusions. The curtains parted to reveal an exotic Persian setting, complete with a savage lion pacing angrily behind the bars of a cage. As the drama unfolded, a beautiful young princess, the sole survivor of a recent shipwreck, found herself forced to choose between becoming the bride of an evil pasha or facing certain doom in the lion's den. Only Lafayette, hurrying to the rescue on a splendid Arabian steed, offered any hope. Then, at the last possible moment, the menacing lion was miraculously transformed into Lafayette himself.

Night after night, audiences thrilled to the magical drama, although sometimes the peril became all too real. Backstage one evening in 1903 at the Grand Opera House in Indianapolis, for example, Lafayette's lion seized one of the magician's beloved dogs. Armed only with a blank pistol, Lafayette charged the beast. The lion dropped the dog but instantly sprang across the stage at Lafayette, knocking him unconscious to the floor. The magician suffered a number of serious bites and ⟳

scratches before his assistants were able to drive the creature off with glowing fire pokers.

Though willing to brave a lion to save a dog, Lafayette was helpless when his adored Beauty died on May 4, 1911, during a tour of Scotland. Tears flowed down his cheeks as he performed that evening at Edinburgh's Empire Theatre. "I have lost my dearest friend," he wrote. "I know that I shall not be much longer in this world." Beauty was embalmed and placed in a luxurious glass-lidded coffin.

Four days later, at the conclusion of the Lion's Bride drama, a decorative stage lamp burst into flames high above the magician's head. At once the entire stage filled with fire. As the asbestos curtain lowered, an alert musician named Wheelan took the stage to play the national anthem, calming the crowd and ensuring their orderly exit from the theater. The act of heroism cost him his life.

Ten others died in the blaze, including Lafayette himself. Witnesses reported that the magician had found his way safely to the street but darted back into the theater to save his animals. His badly charred body, identifiable only by the costume sword he wore, was discovered near the lion's cage. Although Lafayette's lawyer was puzzled not to have found the performer's distinctive diamond rings among these remains, he allowed the body to be cremated, in accordance with Lafayette's last wishes.

But the following day, another body was discovered beneath the stage, wearing the magician's rings on its seared fingers. Suddenly it became clear that the first corpse had been that of Dick Richards, Lafayette's secret double. Houdini himself saw the incident as a fitting epitaph, remarking that Lafayette had fooled his admirers "in life and in death," adding, "I envy him." The real ashes of the Great Lafayette were consigned to an Edinburgh cemetery, where they lie buried in an urn set between Beauty's two front paws. □

The Great Lafayette poses with his beloved mongrel, Beauty, with whom he was buried in Edinburgh.

A Magician at War

After the outbreak of war in 1939, Jasper Maskelyne, one of Britain's most prominent magicians, proposed that the principles of magic and stagecraft be applied to the theater of battle. "War magic and theatrical magic," he wrote, "are very similar things. If I could stand in the focus of powerful footlights and deceive attentive and undisturbed onlookers separated from me only by the width of the orchestra pit, then I could most certainly devise means of deceiving German observers a mile away or more, or perhaps 15,000 feet up in the air, or on Nazi warships at sea." The idea, he believed, was to put the vanish to work on a vast scale, causing whole armies to disappear and forces to spring up where none really existed.

Maskelyne was the perfect man for this ambitious undertaking. He came from a long line of conjurers; his father had also been a famous magician, and his grandfather had established the distinguished Maskelyne and Devant Egyptian Hall, home of some of the world's finest magic shows. With his war magic, however, Jasper Maskelyne knew that he was proposing a performance very different from anything his forebears could have imagined.

In 1940, as German forces prepared for an invasion of England, Maskelyne applied all of his cunning to deceive their military intelligence. As a second lieutenant in the Royal Engineers, he created thousands of lightweight, portable dummy guns carefully designed to throw the correct shadows and leave the proper tracks in the dirt.

Soon Maskelyne created dummy soldiers to operate his dummy guns, and he moved the cardboard men back and forth on wires for the benefit of German spotter planes. When the ersatz batteries had done their job at one location, Maskelyne and his team of assistants simply folded them up, loaded them onto a truck, and set them up somewhere else. The fakes served with distinction, drawing enemy aircraft into isolated areas, where their bombs did little harm. Maskelyne, meanwhile, worked to vanish Britain's genuine armaments into innocuous sheepfolds and pubs. "England," he reported afterward, "put on the biggest magic show in history."

Soon Maskelyne's services were required on other fronts. In North Africa he and his so-called Magic Gang produced whole troops of men and entire divisions of menacing tanks from little more than wood and canvas. The magician ◊

even managed to launch a 700-foot battleship cobbled together from scavenged material. It finally sank, but not before convincing the enemy that Britain had a new dreadnought in the Mediterranean.

While these deceptions spun the illusion of huge forces in the field, Maskelyne set about vanishing the army's real tanks and antiaircraft guns by dressing them as trucks and transports. As the war dragged on, the increasing scarcity of material forced the Magic Gang to improvise with whatever came to hand. Once, they fashioned a crude but effective supply of camouflage paint from several drums of ruined steak sauce and a generous measure of camel dung.

Maskelyne's grandest effect came when he vanished Alexandria harbor. A vital supply point for the Africa campaign, the Egyptian port had been mercilessly pounded by nearly constant bombing raids. Maskelyne's solution was to under-

take a small deception on an enormous scale: He transformed a smaller bay, roughly a mile away, into a scaled-down replica of Alexandria harbor, complete with surrogate landmarks, dummy ships, searchlights, and facades of buildings to fool aerial navigators as they approached the port. When German bombers took the bait, pyrotechnics on the ground gave the illusion of return fire. The ruse worked, and the German bombs obliterated Maskelyne's illusory installation—leaving the genuine port untouched.

But Maskelyne's own finest hour came in the deserts of Africa as General Bernard Montgomery squared off for his decisive battle with Field Marshal Erwin Rommel's Afrikakorps at El Alamein. While he was transporting four dummy tanks across the

desert, the magician suddenly found his group in the path of an advancing column of German armor. He positioned his small squadron of fake tanks, then drove wooden posts coated with reflective paint into the sand nearby. As the German tanks drew closer, Maskelyne prayed that the enemy commanders would spot the sunlight glinting off of his carefully deployed shiny posts and mistake them for gun turrets.

After a tense face-off, the German panzers withdrew, apparently convinced that a massive tank force waited for them in the distance. A relieved assistant asked Maskelyne, "Captain, what would you have done if it was overcast?" The war magician thought for a moment before replying, "A disappearing act." □

In wartime North Africa, Maskelyne's Magic Gang uses artful camouflage to transform an armored car into a harmless truck.

Now You See It . . .

For almost as long as humans have made war, they have used camouflage, a variant of the vanish, to confuse the enemy. Practiced as a deceitful art for centuries, this form of deception has become a virtual science in modern times.

World War I ushered in aerial observation and new weapons of mass destruction, and it gave a new boost to military illusion. The warring armies doffed their colorful battle dress in favor of muted uniforms that blended in with the surrounding terrain. The French experimented with painted coverings to disguise gun batteries, and they established a department of *camouflage* (the word means "disguise") within their army.

Pondering the U-boat menace, a Royal Navy officer named Norman Wilkinson came up with a novel way to avoid enemy torpedoes. He convinced the admiralty to let artists decorate warships with streaks and stripes of paint; they called it "dazzle painting." Ships marked with these bold strokes did not disappear into the background but seemed instead to have an altered shape, making it harder for attackers to judge the speed and direction of their targets.

When World War II exploded, painted camouflage bloomed on tanks, airfields, and factories. In 1942, the Germans began disguising their massive fortifications on the French side of The Channel as harmless villages and farms, and Lockheed Aircraft's California plant was disguised as a residential suburb *(above)*. On both sides of the conflict, camouflage experts built dummy airfields, shipyards, and armored units, and they painted airplanes, ships, and tanks with dapples, free forms and stripes, hoping to vanish their forces under the enemy's very eyes. □

Anchors Away

The U.S. Navy has been credited with many feats, but one of the strangest—and least credible—is that it briefly vanished one of its own warships during World War II. The Philadelphia Experiment, as the alleged disappearance is popularly known, is said to have occurred at that city's port in October 1943. According to the one person who claimed to have observed the incident, an American destroyer at dock was suddenly surrounded by a green haze extending a hundred yards from each side of the ship. Then the vessel disappeared, leaving only the impression of its hull against the ocean. A few minutes later, the ship reportedly appeared at the naval base in Norfolk, Virginia, more than 200 miles away. Then it allegedly vanished again and reappeared in Philadelphia.

The eyewitness was a shadowy figure named Carlos Miguel Allende, who sometimes called himself Carl Allen. Allende claimed later that he had seen the eerie vanishing act from the SS *Andrew Furuseth,* the steamer on which he served as a merchant seaman. He also said that he had put his arm into the strange aura. According to Allende, two of the crewmen aboard the destroyer burst mysteriously into flames, and another flickered back into invisibility. Most of the survivors, he claimed, later went insane.

Allende's tale came to light in 1956 in a series of bizarre letters he sent to Maurice K. Jessup, an astronomer and author of a book called *The Case for the UFO.* Although a small coterie of enthusiasts continues to insist on the truth of the Allende account, the Navy's Office of Naval Research has steadfastly denied any such incident or any research into invisibility. In fact, Allende's is the only "eyewitness" report of the bizarre effect, and there is no other evidence that it occurred. The Philadelphia Experiment appears to be totally an illusion. □

The USS *Eldridge,* a fully manned destroyer escort, was alleged by some to have been the vessel involved in a secret wartime Navy experiment.

Invisible Wings

Just before dawn on Wednesday, December 20, 1989, the silence around the Panamanian barracks at the coastal military base of Rio Hato was shattered by a series of large explosions that plowed up a field nearby. Disoriented and confused, the soldiers had no sense of where the bombs had come from. Their radar showed no aircraft in the area, and they had heard nothing before the detonations broke the stillness. By the time they recovered from their surprise, legions of American paratroopers were on the ground at Rio Hato, and the barracks was quickly neutralized.

The Panamanian Defense Force regulars had been duped by a new kind of vanish, fashioned in the near-legendary Skunk Works at Lockheed Aircraft Company in Burbank, California. More than a decade earlier, engineers there had begun developing an attack plane built around a new technology called Stealth. The resulting fighter, the F-117A, was not acknowledged until five years after it became operational in 1983, and the brief attack on Rio Hato was its first use in combat.

Wobbly Goblin, as the F-117A is called by those who fly it, marked a new era in military deception—rendering aircraft invisible to the electromagnetic eyes of modern warfare. It was joined in 1988 by the Northrop B-2 heavy bomber *(above)*, a modern variant of the 1940s-vintage Flying Wing. For both Stealth aircraft, the designers concentrated on hiding the air-

planes from the electronic pulses of radar and the heat-detecting "noses" of infrared sensors.

Radar works by sending out a radio signal that bounces off an object and returns to the sender. The more direct the bounceback, the bigger the reflection, or radar cross section, which is often many times larger than the original object. For example, a military aircraft such as the bulky B-52 bomber shows a radar cross section of some 10,000 square feet. For the

B-2, it is said to be about the size of a large bird, and for the F-117A, not much more than a BB pellet.

Some techniques for cutting down those profiles have been known for decades. In World War II, the British built an all-wooden bomber, the Mosquito, because they knew wood did not show up on radar. The Germans had their own equivalent, the Horton-9.

The dramatic change in radar profile in the B-2 was achieved by designing the plane as a huge, ⊅

sweptback wing spanning 172 feet with no tail fin, a low-slung, rounded-dome cockpit, and engines built into the top of the aircraft to mask the turbines. The surface of the wing is composed of complex curving shapes, and the trailing edge is crimped like a bat's, further scattering radar signals. The smaller F-117A also has sharply swept wings (span: 40 feet), but its upper surface is composed of sloping, angled straight lines, and it has a tail fin, though not a conventional one.

In both cases, the theory is the same: Smooth or angled surfaces scatter incoming radar beams, reducing the amount of energy reflected back to the sender. And burying the engines within the fuselage or wing dilutes the hot engine exhaust gases that are a beacon for infrared sensors.

Special materials are vital to the invisibility effect. The planes are not made of metal but of materials called composites—carbon-and-fiberglass or plastic-and-fiberglass compounds that absorb radar energy rather than reflect it. The aircraft wings are probably covered with special radar-absorbing paint. The leading edges of the Stealth wings are also built in a special way to sop up radar waves. They are composed of small, hexagonal tubes, similar to honeycombs, each tube filled with materials that absorb radar signals. When a pulse strikes the wing, it is bled of increasing amounts of energy by the tubes, sending a diminished radar echo back in a scattered fashion that weakens it still further.

Although such techniques make it possible to vanish the airplanes as far as enemy sensors are concerned, the bizarre designs are too unstable to fly without the constant attention of complicated and costly computer systems. Indeed, the B-2 is said to cost as much as $850 million per plane, making it by far the most expensive airborne weapon ever fielded. □

LOST WORLDS

Caught in the richly interwoven give-and-take of human history, whole worlds have mysteriously disappeared. For some, the moment of vanishing was abrupt: an epidemic, an earthquake, or a battle. For others, the process was the gradual winking out of a people, the gentle extinction of entire societies over decades and centuries.

Although these vanished worlds can be exhumed and the lives of the people partially reconstructed, it is rare to find a chronicle of the final collapse. The extant shards of pottery and ruined walls and skeletons only now and then reveal the central mystery of these lost worlds: the cause and moment of their disappearance.

Joshua's Wall

A few miles north of the green oasis of modern Jericho is a mound of earth crisscrossed and furrowed by the ditches and excavations of archaeologists. Their initial interest in Jericho centered around the dramatic Old Testament story of Joshua, who led Israelites against the walled Canaanite city sometime between 1550 and 1400 BC and, through divine intervention, overwhelmed the town. In the words of the spiritual hymn, "Joshua fit the battle of Jericho and the walls came tumbling down."

Hoping to locate those tumbled walls, a British archaeological team in 1867 began excavating the hill under which the ruins of the old city were believed to be buried. That expedition, and those that followed, turned up little in the way of results. Then, in the 1950s, a team led by British archaeologist Kathleen Kenyon uncovered a wall much older than the one Joshua had allegedly destroyed. Built in about 8000 BC, the structure was as much as twelve feet high in places, and still solid and free-standing. Its existence indicated that, whatever Jericho might have been in biblical terms, in archaeological ones it was the oldest known city—a city built, according to prevailing preconceptions, before it was humanly possible.

Until this discovery, it was widely believed that prehistoric humans had been nomadic hunters and that cities had not sprung up until the fourth millennium BC. There was no evidence that the cultures of 8000 BC had possessed the mental or technical wherewithal to tend crops on a large scale and accomplish such cooperative works as wall building—prerequisites for forming and sustaining cities.

Beyond the wall's foundation, Kenyon found a trench twenty-seven feet wide and nine feet deep, carved from solid rock. Just within the wall stands a thirty-foot-high, cylindrical tower more than thirty feet in diameter, apparently built at the same time as the wall. Inside the tower, a series of steps descends to near bedrock level, each step made from a single stone, smoothly hammered into place. At the bottom, Kenyon found twelve human skeletons

Archaeologists dug fifty feet into the earth to find Jericho's oldest wall and ancient artifacts that included skulls built up with plaster and given shells in place of eyes.

that were some 9,000 years old.

She also discovered skulls dating from the fifth millennium BC, strangely fitted with plaster masks and seashells in the eye sockets. Each skull had been carefully packed with clay and rebuilt on the outside, apparently to resemble the person's face when alive, for no two of the seven unearthed skulls looked the same. Scientists speculate that the crafted skulls, which have not been found elsewhere, may have been artifacts of ancestor worship, displayed in much the way family photographs are today.

Located at the northern end of the Dead Sea, ancient Jericho encompassed about ten acres and was probably inhabited by two to three thousand people. It appears to have been chosen as a settlement because of a voluminous underground spring that provided life-giving water in an otherwise parched desert valley. The spring still keeps modern Jericho green and fruitful today.

The ancient site was inhabited for more than sixty-five centuries by perhaps ten different cultures. During that time, the city had many walls, some destroyed by quakes, others razed by invaders, still others scattered by the elements during periods when the city was abandoned. Archaeologists have found signs of eleven building phases and of nearly two dozen superimposed floors.

But no trace has been found of the walls immortalized by the Old Testament. Despite indications that the city was once burned, no extant scars can be linked to Joshua's campaign or to the famous wall, which appears to have tumbled into oblivion. □

The Violent End of Crete

From the thirtieth to the sixteenth century BC, a great civilization developed on the Aegean island of Crete. With centers of culture and power in such palatial cities as Knossos, Mallia, and Phaistos, the ancient race was one of skilled seafarers and artisans, an oceangoing people that dominated the Mediterranean for centuries. Then, inexplicably, all of Crete's towns and palaces were destroyed, and the society collapsed, abandoning its former influence and turning away from the sea. Because archaeologists have found echoes of Greek myth in the artifacts and ruins left from that vanished world, they have called it Minoan, after Minos, the legendary Cretan king— and mortal son of the god Zeus—whose palace held the labyrinth and the half bull, half man called the Minotaur. Historians speculate that the Minoans first arrived in Crete about 7000 BC, presumably from Asia Minor. By 1700 BC, the island's population was

an estimated 80,000 to 100,000 people, one of the largest in the world at that time. Expert seafarers and boat builders, the Minoans built sturdy keeled craft that could travel several hundred miles in a few days—this at a time when the Egyptians were using rudimentary troughlike vessels for simple river navigation. Its maritime supremacy so eclipsed that of other cultures that Crete was virtually immune from invasion; the secure Minoans did not even bother to fortify their palaces.

Still, their doom appears to have come from the sea. Around 1500 BC, all of Crete's towns and palaces were ravaged by fire; Minoan civilization was left in ruins. Some scholars originally believed that the great earthquakes of Crete caused the Minoan demise. Others placed the cause with civil unrest or invasion by the warlike Mycenaeans from the Greek mainland. Indeed, there is evidence that after 1500 BC, the Mycenaeans did occupy what ◊

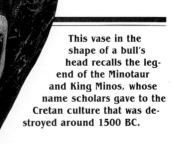

This vase in the shape of a bull's head recalls the legend of the Minotaur and King Minos, whose name scholars gave to the Cretan culture that was destroyed around 1500 BC.

was left of the city of Knossos.

But another group of archaeologists holds that the Minoan destruction came from a distance. About seventy miles north of Crete is a rugged crescent called Santorin, after Saint Irene. With four smaller isles, Santorin describes a shattered ring of rocky outcroppings rising from the sea. Four thousand years ago, these were part of the cone of a great volcano called Thera, with villages settled along its hard flanks until, near the year 1500 BC, Thera literally blew itself apart. Destructive waves called tsunamis struck Crete's coast within half an hour of the eruption; walls of water hundreds of feet high swept well inland, ripping away everything in their path. The fires that destroyed Cretan towns rained down from the sky, along with millions of tons of ash that blotted out the sun and suffocated farms and villages. Its store of lava temporarily exhausted, the volcano caved in upon itself, leaving no trace beyond the islands that still mark its broken rim. □

The Search for Herod's Harbor

Halfway through his reign, King Herod of Judaea embarked on a series of mammoth civil engineering projects. One was a Mediterranean city raised on the ruins of a site called Strato's Tower, where Roman technicians and legions of conscripts raised a new city between 22 and 10 BC. Herod, eager to please his Roman patron, Augustus Caesar, named it Caesarea.

Writing of this feat a little less than a century after its completion, the Jewish historian Flavius Josephus described a technical achievement that seems far beyond the supposed abilities of ancient builders. Somehow, he related, Herod's civil engineers had constructed a capacious fifty-acre harbor along an unstable, sandy coast. Huge stone blocks, about 10 feet on a side and 50 feet long, had been dropped from boats into the 100-foot-deep waters to form a breakwater nearly a mile long, broken only by a narrow entrance for ships. Imposing towers had then been raised along the top of this wall, the tallest of which Herod ingratiatingly named for Augustus Caesar's stepson, Drusus. Colossal statues flanked the harbor's entrance, and Caesarea's skyline of temples, palaces, and theaters filled the eastern horizon beyond the harbor, which Herod called Sebastos—Greek for Augustus.

In later centuries, though, this remarkable structure seemed to disappear from the face of the

An aerial photograph shows the submerged ruins of Herod's harbor as a curved, dark blue mass resting beneath the lighter blue waters of the Mediterranean.

A diver glides over a mosaic floor that once graced a villa near the Roman resort town of Baiae.

earth, and many dismissed Josephus's report as a fabrication. One nineteenth-century antiquary echoed the skeptical consensus when he wrote of the historian's description of Herod's harbor as "grandiloquent hyperbole."

Even so, archaeologists persisted in the search for the lost port. In 1960, divers from an American expedition finally located what seemed to be the remains of the harbor's underwater foundations. But they could not determine for certain that it was the grand facility described by Josephus. Then, in 1976, a new international expedition began a decade-long study of the submerged ruins. Underwater archaeologists soon confirmed that the submerged piles of rubble were indeed the remnants of King Herod's Sebastos.

They also discovered that Herod's engineers, knowing little of geology, had made a crucial error in siting the harbor. For although it endured for a century or two, Sebastos was doomed from the time of its construction. It had been built along a major fault, or crack, in the earth's crust. As slabs of rock moved along this structural break, the harbor was slowly but inexorably shuttled into the sea.

The inevitable collapse was forestalled for a time by constant dredging and breakwater repair. But after Herod's rule, subsequent administrations were less careful. By the harbor's 500th year, ships had begun to founder on the submerged pilings of the sunken breakwater. In the early sixth century AD, the orator Procopius described the residents of Caesarea watching helplessly as cargo-laden ships sank upon trying to enter the once-glorious harbor. ☐

Watering Place

Located near Naples on the Gulf of Pozzuoli, Baiae was ancient Rome's counterpart of modern-day Monte Carlo. Magnificent pavilions were built out on the sea atop raised foundations. Expansive villas dotted the coastline, and marble statues of deities graced the cobblestone streets. Named by the Greeks after Baios, helmsman of the legendary Ulysses, Baiae was also famous for its sulphur springs, said to relieve arthritis and rheumatism. The city had also earned a reputation for satisfying the vacationing Roman's every appetite.

But this "favored city of the emperors," as one historian called Baiae, largely vanished from human view, the victim of a phenomenon that has plagued the coastal cities of Italy for centuries. Some legends liken Baiae's fate to that of the biblical Sodom and Gomorrah, destroyed by divine powers as punishment for their inhabitants' evil ways. But its demise stemmed from a purely geological process called bradyseism, a combination of volcanic activity and subterranean erosion. The seafloor along Italy's west coast is part of the so-called Phlegraean Fields, a honeycomb of volcanic chambers that release hot gases and mud, causing the coastline above to shift.

Usually, the seismic action works slowly, moving land almost imperceptibly up or down over long intervals of time. Such changes doubtless frightened the Romans and led to Baiae's gradual evacuation. Then, in 1538, the volcano Monte Nuovo erupted, and overnight, the remains of the Roman resort—and miles of shoreline—slipped into the sea, where it endures today beneath ten to fifteen feet of water.

But nothing is forever along Italy's volcanically active coast. In 1983, a series of earthquakes and volcanic action lifted the seafloor at nearby Pozzuoli, across the bay, raising the ruins of an ancient Roman market that had been inundated only eight years before. Perhaps the forces that submerged it will one day restore ancient Baiae to the light. ☐

A sandstorm rolls
toward the excavat-
ed ancient city wall
of Dura-Europos in
the Syrian Desert.

Sandbag

In 1921, British troops operating in the Syrian Desert accidentally discovered the ancient city of Dura-Europos, a caravan outpost first established by the Babylonians in 300 BC. During excavations carried out between 1928 and 1937, archaeologists unearthed a synagogue in amazingly pristine condition. The walls were covered with some fifty-eight vivid paintings depicting Moses at the burning bush and receiving the Ten Commandments, as well as other biblical scenes. The colorful tempera murals looked almost freshly painted. But more than the dry desert air had preserved them: A hard-pressed Roman commander inadvertently saved them seventeen centuries earlier by turning the synagogue into a giant sandbag.

Because it was a strategic outpost along the Euphrates River trade route, Dura-Europos was frequently attacked and occupied by different forces over the centuries.

In the third century AD, a declining Roman Empire maintained a tenuous hold on the city in the face of a series of attacks by a new dynasty of Persians called the Sassanians. Alarmed, the desperate leader of the Roman garrison hatched a plan to strengthen the city's defenses.

Noting that the back wall of the synagogue faced the vulnerable west wall of the city, he began to fill the intervening street with sand. That step completed, he had his workers rip away the synagogue's roof and fill the inside of the building with sand to buttress the strengthened outer wall.

His efforts proved futile. In AD 256, the Persians defeated the Romans and sacked the city. Those who didn't manage to escape were probably massacred or sold into slavery. Then, for reasons lost to history, the Persians abandoned the city, leaving untouched the thick, sand-filled enclosure housing art that preserved the vanished ambiance of this ancient world. □

Forgotten

Perhaps Henri Mouhot, the French naturalist, was pursuing local rumors of strange ruins hidden in the forest, or perhaps he had ventured into the Cambodian jungle lured by the rare butterflies that were his passion. Whatever his purpose on that day in 1860, Mouhot made a revolutionary discovery. Half concealed in the dense undergrowth lay an enormous sculpted head. When Mouhot explored further, he found himself among the tumbled towers and partially buried causeways of a splendid ancient city.

Huge roots had burst stone walls, wild orchids ran rampant over gates and spires, and monkeys swung and chattered from clambering vines. Everywhere hung the smell of decay. Nevertheless, Mouhot recognized the ruins for what they were: the remains of a magnificent community of great temples rivaling those of ancient Athens and Rome. Mouhot had discovered Angkor, once capital of the great Khmer Empire. At its

height, the empire encompassed present-day Cambodia and parts of Vietnam, Thailand, and Laos.

In a world where kings were gods, Angkor was the religious and political heart of the vast Khmer realm. Covering thirty-eight square miles, the site was a stunning landscape of shrines and terraces, reservoirs and canals, ballustraded causeways, and temples. One vast section called Angkor Wat, built in the twelfth century by King Surya-varman II, covers a square mile of ground and may be the world's largest religious structure. Bayon, a nearby temple, is noted for its extensive sculptural friezes, which depict marketplaces, mothers with children, and hundreds of other scenes from daily life.

Arising late in the ninth century, Angkor flourished for some three hundred years before entering a period of gradual decline. Then, in 1431, it fell to the Thais. The Khmer abandoned their capital city for Phnom Penh. The empire un-raveled, and Angkor was swallowed up by the jungle.

Why did the mighty Khmer Em-pire collapse in the face of a Thai invasion? Today, most scholars think that the rulers' preoccupa-tion with warfare and the building of great temples caused them to neglect the complex irrigation sys-tem that sustained Khmer rice fields. Without sufficient water, the soil quickly grew parched and un-productive in the torrid climate. Hunger and disease must surely have been the result.

But Angkor had not lain entirely undisturbed all those years. In 1585, a Portuguese friar, Antonio de Magdalena, wrote of a Cambodi-an king called Satha, who found the ruins while hunting. Satha tried to restore the city, and for a time people lived there once more. But the king never succeeded in reviving Angkor's irrigation system, with its intricate arrangement of reservoirs and canals. Eventually he gave up, and the jungle reclaimed the ancient site.

By the time Mouhot rediscovered Angkor, not even local legend re-called the glorious days of the Khmer Empire. When the French-man asked Cambodian villag-ers where the twice-lost, twice-found ruin came from, they shrugged and replied, "It is the work of giants," or, "It made itself." □

The roots of a fig tree embrace a stone Buddha near Cambodia's ancient temple complex of Angkor Wat, depict-ed below by a nineteenth-century French artist.

Seven Wonders of the Ancient World

In the second century BC, the Greek poet Antipater of Sidon compiled a list of the great wonders of his world. His choices were the marvels of antiquity, grand in size, ambitious in design, and beautiful to see. Today, Antipater's seven wonders exist mainly as flickering archaeological memories, for all but one of them have disappeared.

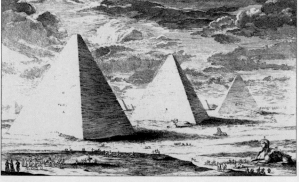

1. The Great Pyramid of Giza. The royal tomb of Cheops had been standing for two thousand years before any of the other marvels was built, and it is the sole survivor among Antipater's seven wonders.

2. The Hanging Gardens of Babylon. Constructed in the seventh century BC near what is today the city of Baghdad, the gardens did not actually hang but instead were constructed in tiers that rose like a small mountain, holding a variety of shrubs, fragrant flowers, and fruit-bearing trees. An extant desert ruin may be a remnant of their irrigation apparatus.

3. The Statue of Zeus at Olympia.
Completed in 456 BC, the 40-foot statue presided over the ancient Olympic games. The giant ivory and gold figure occupied a throne of gold set with ebony, ivory, and precious stones. The games were banned in AD 391, and the site later destroyed by early Christian emperors of Rome. Nothing remains of this statue of the god.

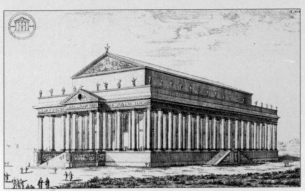

4. The Temple of Artemis at Ephesos.
Said to have been commissioned by King Croesus of Lydia, famous for his great wealth, the temple was built and rebuilt five times, beginning as early as 800 BC. The last was plundered by the Goths around AD 260, and no trace of it can be found today.

5. The Tomb of Mausolus at Halicarnassus.
Upon the death of King Mausolus of Caria in 353 BC, his widow, Artemisia, commissioned a matchless memorial. Although she died two years later, the 140-foot-high tomb was completed in 350 BC, an elegant columned structure of marble, sculpted with lions, standing figures of gods, goddesses, charioteers, and warriors astride horses. It survives only in the generic term it inspired: *mausoleum.*

6. The Colossus of Rhodes.
Said to be the largest and most perfect model of a human figure ever constructed, the 120-foot bronze statue of Helios, the sun god, was toppled by an earthquake in 226 BC, only fifty-six years after its completion. Because an oracle forbade its repair, the great statue lay on the ground until conquering Arabs sold it to a Syrian scrap merchant in about AD 654. Not a fragment remains.

7. The Lighthouse at Alexandria.
Built in the third century BC on the offshore island of Pharos, it rose more than 400 feet to a platform where a fire burned continuously, its light magnified by a "transparent stone"—probably highly polished metal sheets. Damaged by pillaging Arabs in the seventh century AD, the marble-faced structure was destroyed by a series of earthquakes in the late 1300s.

Markings on this fragment of an ox shoulder blade are the earliest known examples of Chinese writing.

Dragon Bones

A possibly apocryphal tale tells of how the scholarly Wang I-Yung, dean of Hanlin College in the city of Peking, came to discover the secret of the dragon bones and illuminate a part of the remote Chinese past that had vanished into legend years before. In 1899, when Wang's family came down with the chills and fever of malaria, their doctor prescribed a concoction containing decayed tortoise shell—fragments popularly called dragon bones—which the patient was expected to grind himself. Wang was intrigued by the compound that was subsequently delivered to his house, for the fragments of turtle shell were covered with markings that had to be some sort of writing.

According to the view then prevailing, prehistoric China had been ruled by several dynasties, but only the last, called the Chou, was well documented by artifacts and records. The preceding dynasty, called Shang, was regarded by most scholars as nothing more than myth. But the inscriptions noticed by Wang I-Yung suggested that the supposedly legendary Shang dynasty had really existed.

For years, the merchants who sold the dragon bones to doctors and curio collectors guarded their secret sources jealously. Finally, in 1910, scholars learned that the shells came from around the city of Anyang in the Henan province of eastern China. The notion of digging into the ground to learn about ancient history was anathema to most of Wang's fellow scholars, for an educated Chinese man was not supposed to dirty his hands with manual labor. But in 1928, the Chinese government broke with tradition, authorizing a full-scale archaeological dig at the Anyang site. Directing the project was Li Chi, who combined both Eastern and Western approaches to scholarship: His classical Chinese education had been capped with a Harvard doctorate in archaeology.

Li's excavations revealed that Anyang was once the capital of the Shang dynasty, which flourished from about 1750 to 1100 BC. Great Shang, as it was called, boasted a palace ninety-two feet long, flanked by workshops where skilled artisans once made exquisite porcelains and ornamented bronze bowls. Underground corridors lined with skeletons hinted grimly at human sacrifice.

Decades of further digging at Anyang yielded about 100,000 inscribed "dragon bones," from tiny fragments to whole turtle shells, and inscribed cattle shoulder blades *(above)*. The bones, scholars discovered, were actually used as oracles in Shang society, and the inscriptions were questions and answers about every aspect of life, from warfare and marriage to health and the planting of crops. Pieced together and translated, the oracle bones offered an extraordinary glimpse into everyday life in China more than 3000 years ago and restored a vanished dynasty to its prehistoric throne. □

Iconoclasts

In 1945, guided by reports of a giant stone eye watching passersby from the jungle, Smithsonian Institution archaeologist Matthew Stirling began the excavation of San Lorenzo Tenochtitlán, an ancient site, in the gulf lowlands of Mexico. The object he unearthed was typical of carvings made by an ancient Mexican people known to archaeologists as the Olmec: a great head more than six feet high, weighing several tons. First discovered in Mexico in the 1860s, the heads are crowned with helmets that resemble those worn by modern American football players and are believed to be the visages of Olmec rulers. The figures have strikingly Negroid features, which led one nineteenth-century discoverer to surmise that Africans must have lived in Mexico during "the first epic of the world." Whatever its origin, this ancient civilization, believed to be the first in the Americas, vanished utterly—even its real name disappeared—except for the distinctive carvings left behind in the jungle.

The large figures have been found at several locations in the steamy rain forests of southern Veracruz and Tabasco. Radiocarbon dating, a technique that became available to archaeologists in 1957, proved that the ancient race had arisen around 1160 BC, long before the Maya. Discoveries at sites such as San Lorenzo in Veracruz revealed that the Olmec were extraordinary engineers, capable of creating an artificial plateau and a complex system of aqueducts. But they are best known for their sculptures: jade statuettes of ball players, great kneeling figures of

Six feet tall, this stone Olmec head was desecrated and ceremonially buried nearly three thousand years ago.

stone, ceramic infants with the faces of snarling jaguars, immense stone altars or thrones embellished with carved figures—and the colossal heads.

The basalt from which the heads and altars were fashioned had to be hauled from the Tuxtla Mountains, some thirty miles northwest of San Lorenzo. Armies of workers must have sweated and strained, dragging boulders down the mountains, loading them onto balsa rafts, floating them down one river to the sea and then up another stream to San Lorenzo. Yet, after the enormous effort that went into their creation, the colossal heads and other sculptures there were systematically desecrated, then ceremonially concealed from view.

In a burst of fury sometime around 950 BC, stone figures were decapitated, the faces of colossal heads were gouged with symmetrically arranged pits, and large pieces were hacked out of altars. (Nearly all of the sculptures found at San Lorenzo had been willfully damaged.) The battered figures were then laid to rest on beds of red gravel and buried in lines within man-made ridges of earth. Some gigantic carvings were hoisted into the air and dropped to smash other statues. The destruction and burial of the monuments were feats almost as extraordinary as the original creation.

Scholars continue to debate why the culture that carved the figures took such heroic steps to eradicate them. Some suggest the sculptures were broken as part of a religious rite of destruction and renewal, or as a form of ritual sacrifice.

But Yale University's Michael Coe, a leader in the field of Mexican archaeology, postulates that Olmec society underwent a catastrophic upheaval that triggered the violation of the altars and statues. He suspects a sweeping overthrow of the ruling dynasty may have been fueled by the rage of the peasants, who had been forced to build the works and move the massive stones. Perhaps, he theorizes, rebelling slaves marred and buried the sculptures as hated reminders of the old order. "I think it is rather like putting the heads of traitors in England on railings and exhibiting them," Coe has remarked. "The Olmec liked to feel, I think, that all of the destroyed heads were under these mounds. . . . It gave them a feeling of accomplishment to have them in there—and, of course, they wouldn't have to look at their predecessors all the time!" □

An excerpt from *An Account of Things Yucatán* published in 1566, shows Bishop Diego de Landa's attempt to relate the Spanish alphabet to the Mayan hieroglyphic script.

A Phantom Alphabet

On stone columns, on ceramic bowls, and in bark-paper books known as codices, the Classic Maya left written messages for posterity. But until the middle of the twentieth century, no one knew how to read them. The key to the Mayan hieroglyphic code appeared to have disappeared with the ancient culture. In fact, it waited in a long-neglected book by a sixteenth-century Spanish missionary.

Assuming that the Mayan writing system was based on an alphabet similar to that used in Spain, Diego de Landa, third bishop of Yucatán, questioned a literate Maya about the "letters" his people used. After what must have been a frustrating session for both men, the priest compiled a list he believed to be the Mayan alphabet and published it in 1566. Within a century of de Landa's interview, however, the surviving Maya had lost the art of writing their ancient language, rendering the inscriptions and codices meaningless.

De Landa's manuscript came to light in the 1860s, but the latent key still went undetected. By that time, scholars thought that the Mayan glyphs were a form of picture writing and failed to take the friar's alphabet seriously.

But in the 1950s, Soviet scholar Yuri Knorozov finally recognized the value of de Landa's work. The thirty-year-old epigrapher with the Soviet Academy of Sciences in Leningrad realized that de Landa and his informant had been tangled in an intercultural misunderstanding. Each time the friar had asked for a letter of the alphabet, the Maya had responded with the symbol for a syllable. For example, when de Landa asked for the letter *b* (pronounced "beh" in Spanish), he was given the Mayan symbol for the syllable *beh*. Many Mayan words, Knorozov saw, were written by stringing together a series of symbols for syllables, not letters. Although his work went unrecognized for many years, Knorozov had made a crucial intuitive leap in breaking the Mayan glyph code. A succeeding generation of researchers has since largely deciphered the ancient language. But Diego de Landa might have done the same four centuries earlier, had he understood the real secret of the Mayan alphabet: There was none. □

Pillars of Society

Near the end of the eighth century AD, decay crept over the great palaces in the Mayan city of Palenque. When roofs collapsed, no crews of workers sprang to make repairs. Mounds of garbage rose in the courtyards, and no one bothered to clear them away. Amid the tumbled masonry and the debris of long-forgotten meals, the forlorn inhabitants struggled to go about their daily business. Only a century before, Palenque had been a teeming metropolis at the height of its power and grandeur. Hordes of sweating laborers built splendid pyramids and temples. Potters created exquisite bowls and vases, and scribes set down historic records on stone tablets, pottery, and the columns called stelai. Yet, within a century, the social structure of Palenque had collapsed, and the magnificent city fell into ruins.

The decline of Palenque was like the lighting of a long fuse that sputtered through the area in Guatemala, Belize, and Honduras known as the Southern Lowlands. Dozens of cities experienced a similar fate. Although some centers endured longer than others, the high civilization known as Classic Mayan culture unraveled and fell to pieces within a span of four or five generations.

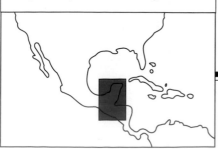

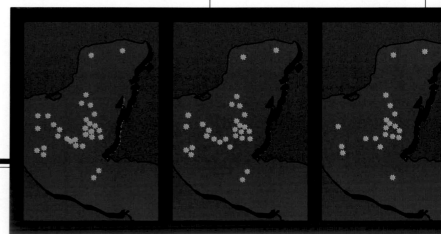

771 - 790   791 - 810   811 - 8

Archaeologists have found one aspect of this vanished society that appears to signal its final decline. In Classic Mayan culture, stelai were inscribed with the history and achievements of the leaders. This practice died out entirely over a period of about a hundred years—the interval, some researchers believe, that marked the irreversible decay of Mayan society.

The last inscription was etched at Palenque in AD 799, at Copan in 820, at Naranjo in 849, and at Tikal in 879. At a few Mayan centers, such as Tonina and Uxmal, these records were still being carved in the early 900s. But by 910, all Mayan cities in the Southern Lowlands had ceased to laud their leaders' exploits in this way.

This spreading cultural silence was a symptom of a wider and still unexplained collapse. Evidence from archaeological digs indicates that the Maya suffered a catastrophic loss of population at the end of the Classic period. Between AD 830 and 930, the Maya were reduced to about one-third of their former numbers. Scientists have speculated that they were decimated by earthquake or hurricane, epidemic, civil war, or invasion. But the true reasons for the collapse vanished with the race.

One scenario recently advanced by archaeologists suggests the Maya may have been the victims not of cataclysms but of their own societal changes. Toward the close of the Classic period, according to this hypothesis, new farming techniques and an improved trade network made food more plentiful than ever before, and the population exploded, nearly doubling in only a hundred years.

Abundance, however, is only an illusion in the jungle, whose impoverished soil cannot sustain crops for more than a few years. Much of the land put under cultivation at this time was originally swamp or rain forest, marginal farmlands that soon lost their ability to feed the growing Mayan population. As food supplies ran short and malnutrition set in, more hands were needed in the fields. But fewer and fewer farm laborers were available because more workers were constantly in demand to build pyramids and temples. As food resources dwindled, competition between Mayan communities increased. An upsurge in warfare further weakened the strained society; when invaders overran some Mayan cities, the people no longer had the power to resist. Like the vine-shrouded ruins they left in the Central American jungle, the Maya slid into decline, less the victims of apocalypse, perhaps, than of their own success. □

For six hundred years the Maya of the Yucatán Peninsula recorded dynastic events on stone columns (below). But during the ninth century, according to university researchers Linda Schele and David Freidel, the practice died out in one Mayan city after another, signaling a cultural beginning of the end. As mapped at bottom, thirty-one cities carved inscriptions during the twenty-year Mayan time cycle that ended in AD 790; by 810, that number was down to twenty-nine and, in successive twenty-year periods, the count steadily declined—to twenty, eighteen, fourteen, thirteen, and, by 890, to three. The last inscription was carved in 909.

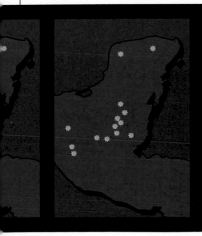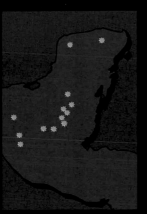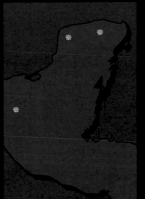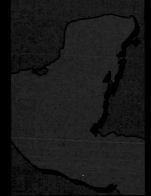

The Wrath of Kan

With its palaces and gleaming temples, broad plazas and opulent burial chambers, the ancient city of Tikal in northeastern Guatemala shines as the very summit of Mayan culture. Yet for decades, scholars have been baffled by an unexplained 135-year gap in Tikal's development as a great metropolis. Inexplicably, part of its history had disappeared.

Beginning in AD 292, the record of royal succession at Tikal flows uninterrupted for some 250 years, in the form of stelai, or stone columns. These pillars, inscribed with hieroglyphic writing and meticulously dated according to the Mayan calendar, trumpeted the accomplishments of one celebrated ruler after another. But suddenly, after the year 557, this record ends. For more than a century no new stelai announce the conquests of Tikal's great leaders, and the tombs of the elite, once splendidly ornamented with jade and shell, become strangely bare. Then, as abruptly as it began, the long silence ends. In 682, stelai once again exalt the city's rulers, recording their lineage and their deeds in carved stone.

The gap had long puzzled archaeologists, who found nothing in the ruins of Tikal to explain the mysterious lapse in development. In fact, the key lay not at Tikal itself, but some forty-five miles to the south, at Caracol, a small Mayan site that, until recently, had been considered insignificant by most archaeologists.

In early 1986, University of Pennsylvania archaeologists Arlen and Diane Chase began full-scale excavations there. The husband and wife team brought different skills to the job; he specialized in Mayan pottery, she in ancient bones. As the two archaeologists cleared underbrush on a Mayan ball court—a paved rectangle where a deadly variant of soccer was once played—Arlen's machete rang against rock. In the middle of the court stood a round stone altar covered by a thin layer of soil. Although it had been cracked and badly eroded by the elements, it bore concentric rings of legible hieroglyphics.

Translated by Steve Houston, an epigrapher from Vanderbilt University, the inscription proved to be the history of Lord Kan of Caracol. The record included the mighty deeds of Kan's father, Lord Water, and recorded a war Caracol waged with Tikal between 556 and 562. Under Lord Water, the once humble Caracol defeated mighty Tikal. By 633, when the altar was carved, Tikal still lay in Caracol's power; the line of Lord Kan had dominated Tikal through the city's long and puzzling silence. □

Circled hieroglyphics on an altar (*above*) record Caracol's victory over Tikal in the sixth century. Temple I at Tikal (*left*) honors Lord Ah-Cacaw, who overcame Caracol in the late 600s.

Incan Retreat

In 1533, the Incan capital of Cuzco fell to Spanish explorer Francisco Pizarro and his followers, who looted the city and stripped the temples of their riches. The king, Atahualpa, was dead, the victim of Spanish treachery. Manco, his half brother, ascended to the throne in name only, the impotent ruler of a ruined, captive empire.

But Manco still burned with a fighting spirit. In 1536, to the consternation of his captors, he escaped and gathered an army of 100,000 men. After an unsuccessful attempt to take Cuzco back from the enemy, he and his forces melted into the remote fastnesses of his mountain kingdom. From a hidden retreat they called Vilcabamba, Manco and his sons waged fierce guerrilla warfare against the Spaniards for the next thirty-six years. Then, according to historians of the day, the Spaniards finally discovered the Incan hideout and sacked it in 1572. Resistance largely disappeared—and so did Vilcabamba.

For centuries afterward, rumors of the lost city teased the imaginations of scholars and adventurers. In 1911, Hiram Bingham, a professor of Latin American history at Yale University, went to Peru, determined to find the legendary stronghold. Retracing the route reportedly taken by Manco when he escaped from Cuzco, Bingham climbed into the high canyon of the Urumbamba River. Along the trail, he met an Indian who promised to show him some interesting old buildings far up the slope.

The climb was so steep, Bingham later wrote, that he frequently had to crawl on all fours, clutching the rocks with his fingernails. At last his guide led him to a saddle between two mountain peaks, where, overgrown with vines and bamboo, an ancient Incan town slept in the sunshine.

The remarkably well-preserved ◊

95

ruin contained some of the finest examples of Incan architecture and craftsmanship the world had ever seen. Most impressive was the horseshoe-shaped Tower of the Sun, facing the sunrise with a breathtaking view over a plunging abyss that dropped to the river more than two thousand feet below. The place was called Machu Picchu, which means "old peak" in Quechua, but Bingham was convinced for the rest of his life that he had found the Vilcabamba of Incan legend.

Yet considerable evidence weighs against Bingham's claim. Machu Picchu was apparently never seen by the plundering Spaniards, and it was far too small to shelter Manco's vast army. Some observers have concluded that, rather than being a lost city, it was a powerful chieftain's mountain retreat.

But, if Machu Picchu was not the stronghold of Manco and his sons, what was? In 1964, American explorer Gene Savoy proposed that another Incan site, sixty miles from Machu Picchu, might be the real Vilcabamba. Called Espiritu Pampa, those ruins reveal fountains, canals, a palace, and almost 300 houses. Though decorated with Incan motifs of birds and serpents, roof tiles were made in the colonial manner, indicating that the buildings were constructed after the Spanish conquest.

Espiritu Pampa is only one of several candidates, however. Until archaeologists find some more compelling proof that one or the other of these ruined towns was once the legendary Incan stronghold, Vilcabamba remains among the missing. It could very well still wait to be discovered somewhere in the mountain forests of Peru. □

Burial Mound

For centuries, the Makah Indians of America's Pacific Northwest have told a harrowing story about the old times in the village of Ozette. One day, as the work of weaving and whale hunting unfolded among the cedar-plank houses near the beach, a terrible cataclysm struck the community. A dreadful roar drowned out the murmur of the sea. Terrified, the people rushed for the doors, mothers snatching up their babies. Scrambling out and away, some managed to escape, as behind them the village disappeared beneath an advancing wall of mud.

The story was part of the Makah's oral history, which speaks of the four thousand years they lived on a beach terrace at Ozette. In the 1920s, they were forced to move away from Ozette so that their children could attend school in nearby Neah Bay. But the old people still told of the great slide that took away their past in a wave of wet clay. Outside the tribe, the story was held to be merely an apocalyptic myth.

In 1970, a severe winter storm sent breakers crashing up the beach to Ozette, ripping away a great slab of the bank. Not long after, a passing hiker noticed a carved wooden object protruding from a pile of mud. It was a canoe paddle, in excellent condition.

When word of his find, and of other objects brought to light by the storm, reached the Makah Indians, they leaped at the chance to explore their former home more systematically. The tribal chairman invited Richard Daugherty, an archaeologist from Washington State University, to conduct excavations

at the site. Daugherty had led other digs in the area and had long suspected that excavations there might be rewarding. But nothing had prepared him for what would be uncovered at Ozette.

Just as the ancient legend said, a great mud slide had smothered Ozette in midgasp. Beneath a layer of earth more than ten feet thick, the vanished village lay locked in a four-hundred-year-old moment, preserved like a fly in amber by the suffocating clay, which shut out the supply of oxygen so completely

that wood, fabric, and bark were preserved from decay. The archaeologists even found green leaves, which turned brown before their eyes when exposed to the air. Although most walls collapsed under the tremendous weight of the mud, Daugherty and his team were able, over the following decade, to piece together a remarkably detailed picture of life in Ozette near the end of the sixteenth century.

They carefully excavated three Makah houses and collected some 60,000 artifacts. He and his team found deadly harpoons, dresses made of cedar bark, and hundreds of boxes carved with the figures of whales, seals, and sea otters. There were wooden bowls that still smelled of seal oil. The archaeologists discovered the skeleton of a puppy, which had died while curled up in sleep. And there were the bones of the men, women, and children who did not escape the catastrophe. Having unearthed the Makah's vanished past, the archaeologists reinterred the bones of the ancient dead for the tribe. □

Preserved for 400 years by suffocating mud, this owl-shaped wooden shaman's wand was found at Ozette, a Makah Indian village opposite the distinctively shaped Cannonball Island *(far left)* on Washington State's Olympic Peninsula.

The Missing Colonists

In 1584, explorers sent to the New World by Sir Walter Raleigh returned to England with accounts of a land that "bringeth forth all things in abundance, . . . without toil or labor." The claims created a sensation. Raleigh won a Parliamentary patent to colonize the land he named Virginia, in honor of his unwed queen, Elizabeth I.

The following year, one of Raleigh's partners, Sir Richard Grenville, led 500 prospective colonists—all men—to the new homeland. The local Roanoke Indian chief, Granganimeo, invited the foreigners to stay on the northern end of Roanoke Island, about 100 miles south of the Chesapeake Bay. A fort was built, the colonists erected houses, and Grenville sailed away, leaving the 108 settlers who had chosen to remain.

Relations with the Roanoke tribe soon began to go downhill. The amiable Granganimeo died, and his brother, Wingina, forbade trading with the settlers. Fearing that Wingina would attack, Ralph Lane, the leader of the remaining colo-

nists, launched a preemptive strike in May 1586. The skirmish killed Wingina but made the settlement's position untenable. In June, a fleet commanded by Sir Francis Drake arrived, fresh from devastating Spanish strongholds in Florida. Leaving a detachment of 15 men to protect the fragile enclave, Drake took the others home.

In July 1587, a new consignment of colonists arrived, led by John White, the chief cartographer on the previous voyage. Among the group of 150 settlers in his charge were 17 women and 6 children, including his married and pregnant daughter, Elenora Dare. Expecting to be welcomed by the compatriots who had stayed behind, they found only silence. Soon after landing they came upon the bones of a settler who had been killed by Indians. The fort had been burned to the ground; the houses were unmarred but deserted. No trace of the other 14 colonists was ever found.

Despite this ominous beginning, the new band decided to stay on at Roanoke but send an expedition south

toward Croatoan Island, where earlier English explorers had befriended the Croatoan tribe. On July 18, 1587, Governor White's daughter gave birth to the first English child born on New World soil, a girl named Virginia. Less than two months later, John White returned to England for supplies, leaving 121 settlers behind. But, delayed by England's war with Spain and other difficulties, White did not return to Roanoke until August 15, 1590, where he found—nothing.

On reaching shore, the relief party found the letters *CRO* carved on a tree. White was looking for

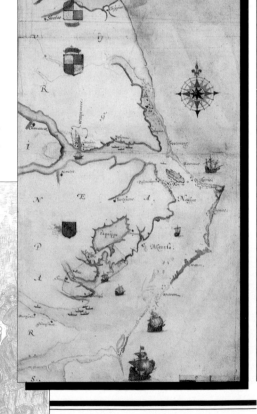

A map drawn by English colonist John White shows Roanoke Island as a pink oval inside the islands of North Carolina's Outer Banks.

Early English colonists to North America brought
armor to the New World, such as these heavy
helmets found at Martin's Hundred in Virginia.

another sign: a cross, which the settlers had agreed to carve in some prominent spot in case of trouble. There was no cross, but the relief group did find that the settlers' houses had been knocked down and replaced by a strong palisade. A tree that formed part of the crude fortress had the word *CROATOAN* carved on it. Inside the fort, a few objects lay scattered. There were no human remains and no signs of violent struggle.

At first, White was relieved. The word on the tree suggested that, as agreed upon before his departure, the colonists had left the name of their next destination. "I greatly joyed," White wrote, "that I had safely found a certaine token of their safe being at Croatoan . . . and the Savages of the Island our friends." But the refusal of his crew to explore further, and a series of storms, forced White back to England before he could confirm this fact. After what appears to have been a final, futile effort to return to America, he gave it up and ended in retirement in Ireland.

His failure to explore beyond Roanoke in 1590 sealed forever the mystery of the colonists, whose fate is still unknown. One theory holds that the group made its way to Croatoan Island and built a ship in which to return home, only to perish at sea. Although the fortification at Roanoke showed no signs of violence, some observers have speculated that Spanish invaders carried off the colonists. And there is evidence that the settlers moved north to the deeper ports offered by the Chesapeake Bay. There, according to the region's powerful Indian chief Powhatan, all remaining Europeans were killed by his warriors fifteen years later. □

Martin's Hundred

The Indian attack against the small English settlement near Jamestown on March 22, 1622, was brief and vicious. When it ended, 58 Europeans were dead. Another 20 were carried off as hostages. Their scattering of homes and outbuildings, which may have rivaled the original Jamestown settlement of 1607 in size, never recovered from the treacherous blow. Within a few years, it vanished completely, its name and location utterly forgotten for three and a half centuries.

The brief history of the small community shows the fragility of the early European settlements in America. Most of the settlers at the tract, located about ten miles downriver from Jamestown, left England in 1618 aboard the ship *Gift of God.* There were about 220

in all, under the auspices of the Virginia Company of London, the private shareholders' group that had founded Jamestown. The 20,000 acre tract that would be home to the *Gift of God* contingent was considered to be a *hundred,* a British term for a unit of land capable of supporting one hundred families. As Richard Martin was the leading shareholder, it was called Martin's Hundred.

Bad luck dogged the venture from the start. Some settlers died on the Atlantic crossing, and the main contingent rested for a time at Jamestown. The ranking officer to survive the voyage, John Boise, was responsible for parceling out land to the settlers. He hurried to establish the first fortified home at Martin's Hundred because the ◊

settlers were concerned about invasion by England's European enemies, Spain and France.

When the settlers finally reached their new home, they numbered about 140. They soon built a larger fort, houses, and a sizable common barn. Their town was named after the most prominent shareholder in their London company, Sir John Wolstenholme (who had backed the ill-fated explorer Henry Hudson in his search for the Northwest Passage). The community began to thrive.

But not everyone was pleased by its success. Watching the colonists, the Indians of the Powhatan Confederacy—led by Chief Opechancanough—were gripped, as one of the surviving colonists later put it, by "the dayly feare . . . that in time we . . . would dispossesse them of this Country." Their solution: an uprising against all the settlements in the Virginia Tidewater area.

When the blow fell, more than twenty communities were attacked, and about 350 Europeans killed. Wolstenholme Towne was among the hardest hit. According to survivors, the Indians disguised their intentions by arriving at the towns unarmed. Some of them even "sate downe at Breakfast." Then, at a signal, the guests grabbed up the tools and weapons of the English and began to kill. A colonist later noted that the attackers were "so sodaine in their cruell execution, that few or none discerned the . . . blow that brought them to destruction." The attackers mangled and scalped many of the corpses.

Among those killed was Richard Kean, the governor's deputy. John Boise was out of town when the attack came and survived; but his servants were killed, and his home destroyed. His wife, listed as dead, was carried off as a hostage and released a year later, "caparisoned like an Indian queen."

The attack destroyed all but two houses at Martin's Hundred and reduced the population to about 62 settlers. More important, it broke the group's spirit. By 1625, only 30 people still lived on the tract. By 1645, according to present evidence, the place was uninhabited. No one knows precisely when the Martin's Hundred plantation faded out of existence. Eventually only the name was left, and even that was altered by usage over time to Merchant's Hundred. When a plantation called Carter's Grove was built near the original town location, even the name disappeared. The original settlement was buried under plowed fields.

The resurrection of Martin's Hundred began in 1969, after the Carter's Grove site became the property of the Colonial Williamsburg Foundation. In 1976, archaeologists searching for eighteenth-century outbuildings to the mansion stumbled upon traces of the older structures. The layout of the housing sites, plus the placement of the barn, convinced them of links between Wolstenholme Towne's plan and English settlements in what is now Northern Ireland, where colonies had been established early in the seventeenth century. Wolstenholme Towne has now been partially reconstructed for the benefit of tourists and historians. Despite death and long obscurity, the Martin's Hundred settlers have outlasted their enemies, for the tribes that so rightly feared the colonists' success have largely vanished. □

GONE FOREVER

Extinction is the disappearance not of an individual or of a community, but of an entire species. It is vanishing rendered absolute and irrevocable. In the four billion years since life began on earth, species have come and gone in vast numbers; more have vanished than now exist. Many succumbed during great waves of extinction that swept away all but a minority of species. But most followed lonely paths to oblivion, unable to adapt to environmental changes that posed little threat to their more flexible contemporaries.

In some instances, like a conjurer's vanished assistant reappearing suddenly among the audience, seemingly extinct species have been discovered alive and well in remote areas. But most life forms that appear to be extinct are just that; they will never be seen in the flesh again. And the harsh selection process is still very much alive. Indeed, some scientists believe the massive wiping out of species has only just begun.

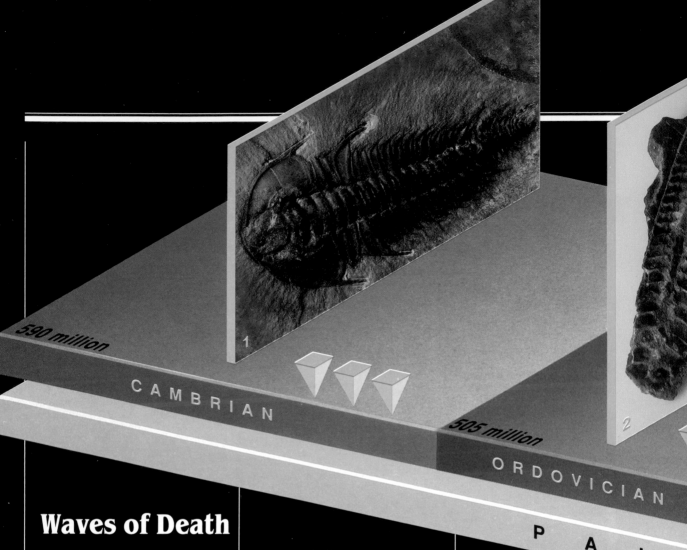

590 million

CAMBRIAN

1

505 million

2

ORDOVICIAN

P A L

Waves of Death

As a grim counterpoint to the vibrant heartbeat of life, episodes of widespread death punctuate the development of earth's living things. Fossil evidence indicates that several mass extinctions have occurred since life first appeared on the planet some four billion years ago. In each of them, a wide variety of species died out in the span of a few million years or less—almost overnight, by evolutionary standards.

Although the cause of these biological cataclysms is unknown, most scientists agree that such wholesale extinctions differ substantially from the ordinary, piecemeal disappearances known as background extinctions. In fact, groups of species, or genera, with

an unusually low background extinction rate—an indication of ecological strength—are often just the ones that are wiped out in a mass extinction.

The first known pulse of extinction took place in the oceans about 650 million years ago when blue-green algae, an ancient life form, were killed off by global cooling. Subsequent extinctions preyed upon more evolved species. Large, armored fish were among the first vertebrate casualties, destroyed about 370 million years ago by something lethal—and still unknown—in their primitive world. Then, some 250 million years ago, the most severe extinction in the planet's history erased most saltwater species and killed off many

of the newly evolved land vertebrates.

From a human perspective, however, the most significant episode was the great dying that began about 65 million years ago and led to the disappearance of many flowering plants, millions of marine species, and virtually every large terrestrial animal, including the dinosaurs that had dominated earth for 130 million years. That vanishing overturned the long reign of reptiles, which were succeeded by smaller, more versatile mammals. One of these mammalian lines would eventually give rise to *Homo sapiens*. □

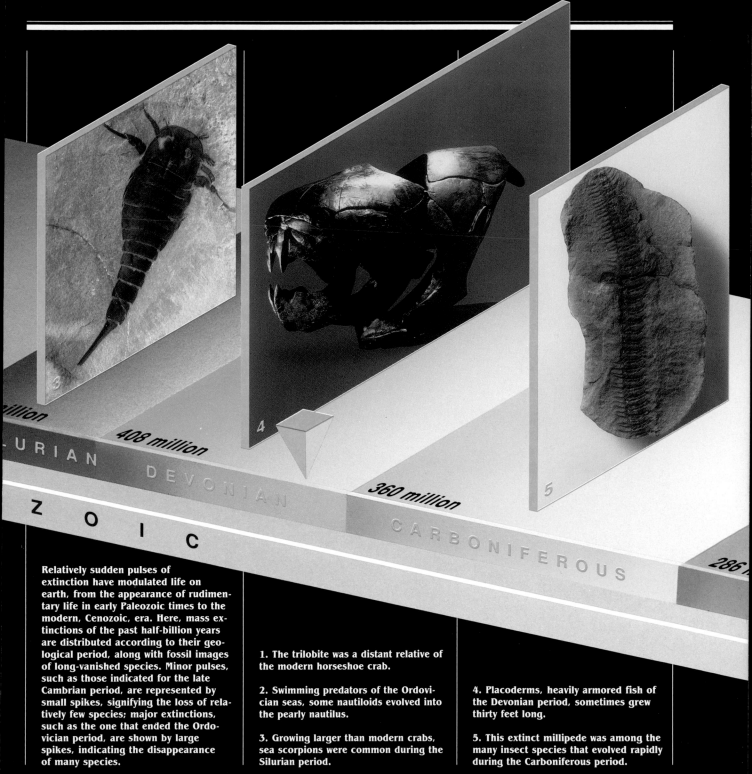

illion

-URIAN   408 million

D E V O N I A N   360 million

C A R B O N I F E R O U S   286 m

Z O I C

Relatively sudden pulses of extinction have modulated life on earth, from the appearance of rudimentary life in early Paleozoic times to the modern, Cenozoic, era. Here, mass extinctions of the past half-billion years are distributed according to their geological period, along with fossil images of long-vanished species. Minor pulses, such as those indicated for the late Cambrian period, are represented by small spikes, signifying the loss of relatively few species; major extinctions, such as the one that ended the Ordovician period, are shown by large spikes, indicating the disappearance of many species.

1. The trilobite was a distant relative of the modern horseshoe crab.

2. Swimming predators of the Ordovician seas, some nautiloids evolved into the pearly nautilus.

3. Growing larger than modern crabs, sea scorpions were common during the Silurian period.

4. Placoderms, heavily armored fish of the Devonian period, sometimes grew thirty feet long.

5. This extinct millipede was among the many insect species that evolved rapidly during the Carboniferous period.

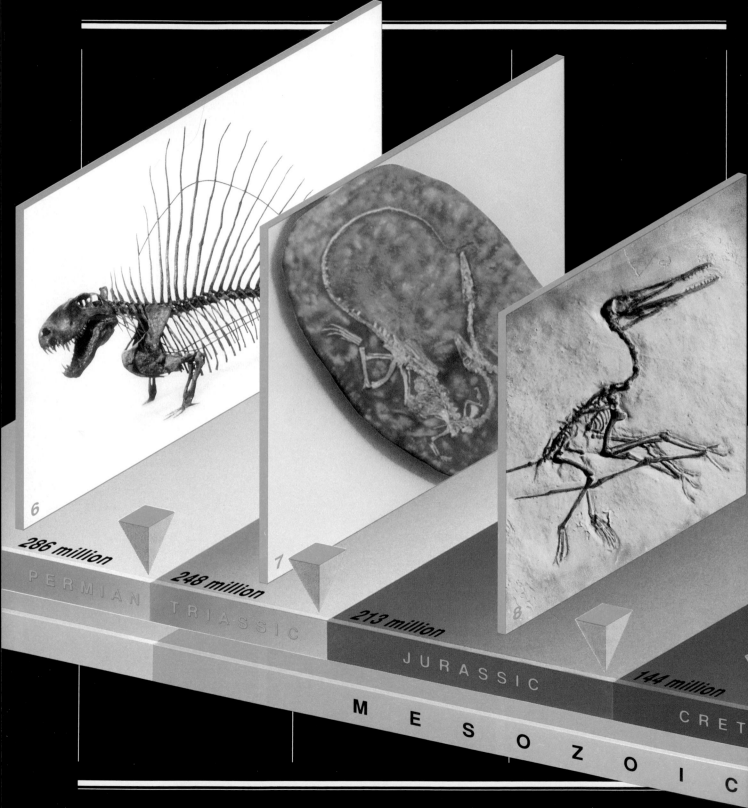

6

286 million

248 million

7

213 million

8

144 million

PERMIAN

TRIASSIC

JURASSIC

CRET

M E S O Z O I C

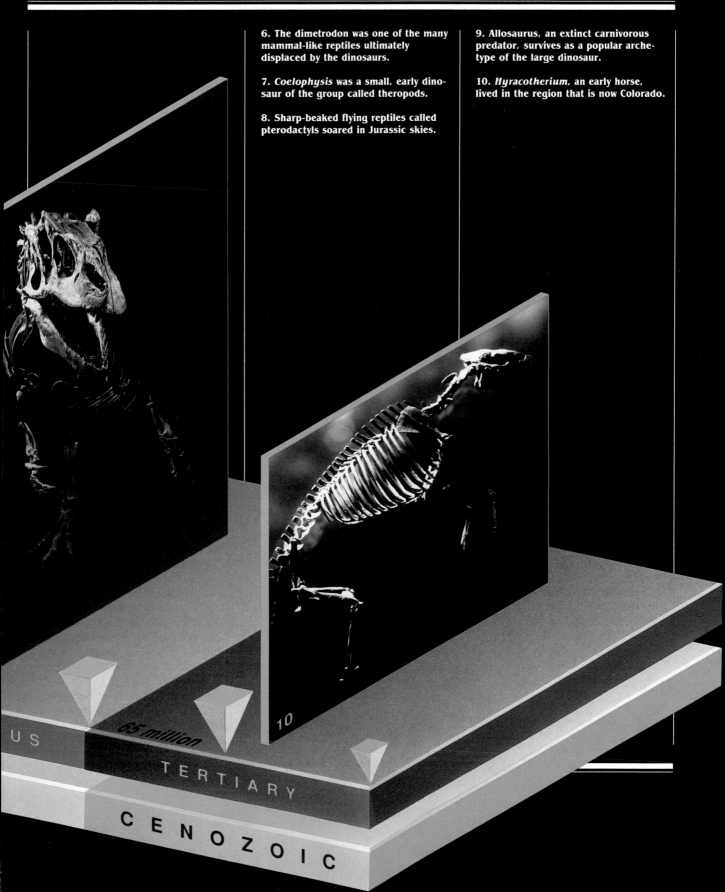

6. The dimetrodon was one of the many mammal-like reptiles ultimately displaced by the dinosaurs.

7. *Coelophysis* was a small, early dinosaur of the group called theropods.

8. Sharp-beaked flying reptiles called pterodactyls soared in Jurassic skies.

9. Allosaurus, an extinct carnivorous predator, survives as a popular archetype of the large dinosaur.

10. *Hyracotherium,* an early horse, lived in the region that is now Colorado.

10

65 million

U S

T E R T I A R Y

C E N O Z O I C

Winterkill

The classic explanation for mass extinctions is that the global environment altered until it became hostile to life forms it had previously supported. Changes in climate, sea level, and ocean circulation are all thought to have played parts, but until relatively recent years there was little understanding of the mechanisms that could produce such radical shifts.

One explanation emerged in the 1960s, when geologists began to accept the theory that earth's land masses are not fixed in place but instead move continuously, breaking apart and joining together to form new continents. The process, called plate tectonics, occurs with almost imperceptible slowness, at a pace of fractions of an inch each year. Although this annual increment is small, over millions of years continents creep great distances, carrying land masses toward and away from the tropics and altering global climate in the process. Glaciers forming on continents near the poles would lock up vast quantities of water, impairing the planet's mechan-

isms of heat exchange and causing a net temperature drop. The ice sheets would reflect sunlight rather than absorb it, further chilling the planet. Such global cooling could decimate life forms that thrive in ordinarily warm tropics. The reverse effect, in which continental movement caused land masses to heat up, would be equally devastating for species adapted to icy polar climes.

But, in the view of some scientists, radical shifts in climatic conditions need not be homegrown. They propose that collisions with meteorites or comets may have triggered global temperature shifts that caused the mass extinctions seen at intervals along the evolutionary trail *(pages 102-105)*. In 1980, Nobel Prize-winning physicist Walter Alvarez and three colleagues at the University of California, Berkeley, found that a layer of sedimentary rock coinciding with a period of mass extinction held unusually high concentrations of iridium. Relatively rare on earth, this metallic element is often abundant in meteorites. Subsequent research detected abnormally high concentrations of iridium in the same geological stratum around the world. The group interpreted the iridium as the residue of fallout from the earth's collision with a titanic meteorite, or bolide.

To produce the cataclysm envisioned by Alvarez and others, such an extraterrestrial body would have to have been about six miles in diameter, traveling at better than ten thousand miles per hour. The collision would have released the equivalent energy of some 60 million one-megaton hydrogen bombs and would have carved out a crater nearly a hundred miles across.

From the point of this enormous impact, a cloud of dust and smoke would have quickly spread around the globe, cutting off sunlight for months. The long darkness and consequent cooling would have been disastrous for plants and animals, particularly for those not adapted to harsh winter conditions. Whole ecosystems of species would have died out before the first weak sunlight began to filter through the clouds again.

Because there are at least a thousand asteroids and comets that cross earth's orbit, one of the size required by Alvarez's theory should hit earth about every 100 million years, on average. Despite this seeming inevitability, the collision theory is not universally accepted as an explanation for mass extinctions.

The vanishing that it explains best is the mysterious disappearance of dinosaurs, one of the most successful races of animals ever to inhabit earth. While excess iridium appears in many rock strata, it is most pronounced in what is called the K-T boundary, the stratum marking the interval between the Cretaceous and Tertiary geological periods some 65 million years ago, when the great reptiles still roamed the planet.

Some researchers believe that the collision and subsequent climatic changes were a coincidence. According to paleontologist Erle Kauffman, a cosmic impact did occur at the end of the Cretaceous. But, he notes, slow climate changes had already begun to destroy the ecosystem that supported the dinosaurs, and the huge reptiles were vanishing with it when the cataclysm that produced the iridium layer occurred. □

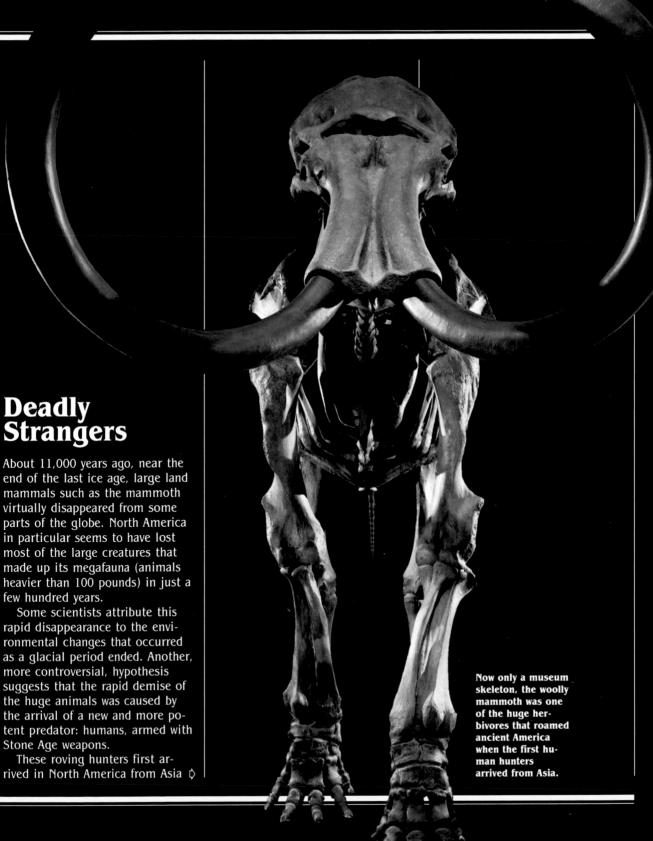

Deadly Strangers

About 11,000 years ago, near the end of the last ice age, large land mammals such as the mammoth virtually disappeared from some parts of the globe. North America in particular seems to have lost most of the large creatures that made up its megafauna (animals heavier than 100 pounds) in just a few hundred years.

Some scientists attribute this rapid disappearance to the environmental changes that occurred as a glacial period ended. Another, more controversial, hypothesis suggests that the rapid demise of the huge animals was caused by the arrival of a new and more potent predator: humans, armed with Stone Age weapons.

These roving hunters first arrived in North America from Asia ◊

Now only a museum skeleton, the woolly mammoth was one of the huge herbivores that roamed ancient America when the first human hunters arrived from Asia.

some 11,000 years ago, after a lower sea level uncovered a land bridge across the Bering Strait. As they made their way southward, the newcomers would have found regions thick with creatures such as the elephantlike mammoths, sloths as big as present-day bears, and bison with horns that spread six feet. For sophisticated hunters with well-crafted weapons, these huge beasts must have been relatively easy prey.

According to Paul S. Martin, the University of Arizona geoscientist who first proposed the theory, even a few hundred hunters and their families in the original migration from Asia would likely have multiplied rapidly in this veritable Eden of game. Martin estimates that if each of the hunters in this expanding population killed an average of one large animal a week, it would have taken only about four centuries to extinguish most species of megafauna. □

Back from Oblivion

The fish that Hendrick Goosen hauled out of the Indian Ocean one day in December 1938 was like nothing he had seen before. Five feet long, the 127-pound creature had large, rough scales; eight fleshy fins; and a square jaw filled with teeth. The South African fisherman took his strange catch to Courtenay Latimer, curator of the local museum. She identified it as a coelacanth, a species believed to have disappeared from the oceans in the distant past.

Latimer called the odd find to the attention of Rhodes University ichthyologist James L. B. Smith, who was familiar with the coelacanth only as a fossil that made its first appearance in rocks about 350 million years old. The antiquity and configuration of the fish suggested to some that the coelacanth might have been a precursor of the amphibians that first crawled from the sea onto land some 365 million years ago. But then, after what seems to have been a long period of worldwide abundance, the species appeared to vanish; it has not been found in rocks younger than about 60 mil-

lion years. Smith noted only very slight evolutionary differences between Hendrick Goosen's catch and the fossil fish, and he generously named the modern species *Latimeria chalumnae* after the perceptive curator who recognized it.

Although scientists were startled by the appearance of this living fossil, the continued existence of coelacanths was no surprise to natives of the Comoro Islands, where more specimens were later found. The islanders were well acquainted with the creature; they ate its flesh, lightly salted, and used its scales as sandpaper. For them, it had never disappeared. □

Once thought to survive only as a fossil *(top)*, living coelacanths were discovered in the Indian Ocean in 1938.

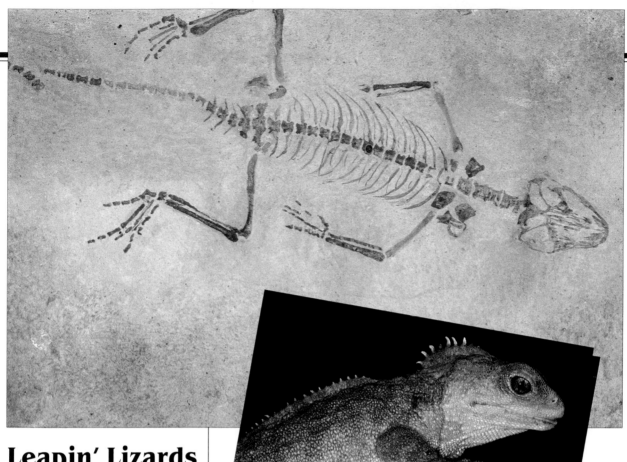

Leapin' Lizards

The first European settlers in New Zealand dismissed the tuatara as just another lizard, of no particular interest for food or skin. But when scientists examined the two-pound creature more closely, they discovered that it was not really a lizard at all: The tuatara was the sole surviving member of the Sphenodons, reptiles that were contemporary with dinosaurs and thought to have been extinct for more than 180 million years.

Virtually unchanged through nearly two million centuries, the tuatara has features that distinguish it from modern reptiles. Perhaps the most unusual is a third eye in a socket atop its head, unable to perceive images but sensitive to light and heat. Scientists believe it functions as a thermo-stat, telling the tuatara when it is time to get out of the sun. Though sluggish and slow to reproduce, the creature is a virtual ball of fire at low temperatures. Other reptiles become paralyzed when the mercury falls much below fifty degrees Fahrenheit. But the tuatara remains active down to forty-three degrees, which may explain why it survived climatic swings that extinguished other reptilian species.

Easy prey to almost any mammalian predator, the tuatara's continued existence depends on isola-tion. They were completely exterminated on New Zealand's two main islands by 1850, wiped out by the rats and other animals that accompanied human settlers. But colonies totaling about 50,000 tuataras survive on small islands off the coast. In these protected outposts, the relic reptiles display remarkable longevity in their own right: Most of them live to an age of sixty or older. □

Sphenodon, whose fossil remains place it in the age of dinosaurs, survives on islands off New Zealand as a single species, the tiny, lizardlike tuatara.

strong and very active physically.

Although a thick browridge gave them a heavy-featured appearance, their brain capacity was about the same as that of early modern humans, and they were probably capable of speech. They used an extensive array of tools and had a simple but well-developed culture. A few Neanderthal graves contain pollen, which is evidence that flowers were interred with the remains. Some skeletons show signs of frequent injury, which indicate caretaking of incapacitated individuals by the group.

Rather than simply writing off the Neanderthals as a dead end in the evolution of humankind, most scholars now believe that they were ancestral to modern man. They hypothesize that Neanderthals intermixed with early modern humans, *Homo sapiens sapiens.* There is evidence in the Middle East, for example, that Neanderthal and Cro-Magnon humans coexisted. Apparently, the more primitive ancestors did not vanish into lonely extinction but into the modern human race. □

Alley Oop

About 32,000 years ago, a primitive human group appears to have vanished rapidly from the face of the earth. Called Neanderthal after the German valley in which their remains were first discovered in 1856, their disappearance from the fossil record was followed shortly by the appearance of a heavily built version of modern humans popularly known as Cro-Magnon. Scientists have no clear explanation for this phenomenon, although several hypotheses have been advanced.

Some argue that Neanderthal's disappearance was a true extinction, the result of a failure to

compete with the more highly evolved humans, descended from African ancestors, who moved into their foraging grounds. But a number of researchers believe that the Neanderthals were too successful for too long to have been so rapidly displaced.

Despite their reputation for being primitives, Neanderthals were well adapted to their environment. They fashioned rudimentary clothing and shelters from animal skins. Bones uncovered around their campsites show that they were skillful hunters, although they still scavenged the kills of larger carnivores. The skeletons of the Neanderthals themselves indicate that they were exceptionally

The Meek

Paranthropus robustus was a contemporary of *Homo erectus,* a direct ancestor of modern humans. With huge cheek teeth and a brain about half the size of the brain of *H. erectus, P. robustus* was long believed to have been a rather unintelligent vegetarian that could not compete with smarter, toolmaking primitive humans.

Analysis of fossils found in a cave at Swartkrans, South Africa, however, indicates that *P. robustus* used stone tools that may have been of its own making. Hand bones show that *P. robustus* had the opposed thumb—a characteristic previously believed unique to *H. erectus*. Furthermore, simple tools found in the area have microscopic wear patterns indicating that they were used over a period of days and that they were transported from place to place by *P. robustus*, perhaps in leather pouches also used to carry food.

There is no indication that *P. robustus* fashioned weapons. More likely, the implements were used to dig out and cut up edible plants. Judging by its foot bones, *P. robustus* did a lot of walking, presumably foraging for food.

Given these signs of resourcefulness, *P. robustus's* extinction is a puzzle for paleontologists. One explanation is that the creature became too dependent on a narrow range of foods that disappeared because of climate changes. Another possibility put forward by some scientists, however, poses a cruel irony: Having foregone hunting and the development of weapons, the meek, ground-dwelling *P. robustus* became easy game for the carnivorous predators of the African savanna. □

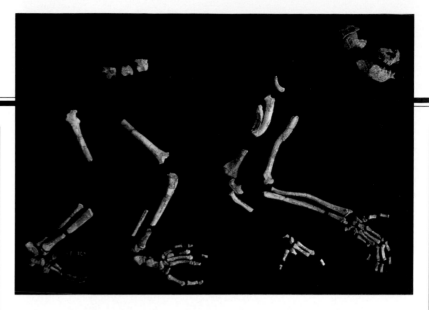

The Missing Link?

In 1927, a settler in western Kenya sent the British Museum an oddly shaped stone that he had found in a limestone quarry. A tooth protruded from the sample, which careful chipping revealed to be part of the left upper jawbone of a hominoid primate, a member of the superfamily that includes humans, the great apes (chimps, orangutans, and gorillas), and the lesser apes (gibbons). Judging by the ages of associated fossils discovered in the quarry, the relic was eighteen million years old—many millennia older than human ancestry was then thought to be.

Intrigued, paleontologist A. Tindell Hopwood of the British Museum went to Kenya in 1931 to learn more about such ancient branches of the human family tree. He found additional hominoid fossils, and in 1933, he published his conviction that the jawbone was of a new genus, an ancestor of the chimpanzee. He named the new ape *Proconsul africanus,* a play on the name of Consul, a famous pipe-smoking chimp that performed at Belview Zoo in Manchester, England, in the late 1800s.

More *Proconsul* bones came to light over the years on an island in Africa's Lake Victoria, but many were not properly identified and found their way into collections of turtle fragments and pig bones. Only in the 1980s, after careful detective work by several paleontologists, were enough pieces assembled to give a clear picture of this extinct ape *(above).* It had a relatively large brain compared to its body weight, a characteristic of the great apes and of humans. It had sinus cavities similar to those of the great apes (absent in the lesser apes), and its pelvic structure suggested that *Proconsul* lacked the ischial callosities, or buttock pads, of the lesser apes. *Proconsul* was a slow-moving creature that lived primarily in trees, probably descending only rarely; it had no special adaptations for life on the ground.

Such patterns of similarity and difference between *Proconsul* and the modern apes led many scientists to conclude that the extinct creature was more than just another vanished precursor to humans. Instead, it could be a long-sought missing link, a common ancestor connecting apes and humans millions of years before they went their separate evolutionary ways. □

Gunning for a Dinosaur

Although erosion and earth movement have brought many fossils into view, most remain entombed below the surface, inaccessible to human view. But, employing recent variations on the technology used to probe the earth's upper layers for oil-bearing formations, paleontologists are taking a sonic look at fossils still interred. One of the most sensational dinosaur discoveries of recent years, in fact, was identified before it was dug from sandstone in the desert canyon land of New Mexico.

Only a few of the ancient creature's tailbones protruded from the sandstone when two hikers came across it in 1979. Painstaking excavation began in 1985, and in the next few years, digging was guided by information gleaned from such remote sensing equipment as radar and magnetometers. The most accurate technique, however, was one that had been developed for finding and charting the burial sites of hazardous wastes.

The technique sends sound waves through the ground to a vertical array of twenty-nine microphones suspended on a wire in a

nearby 20-foot-deep borehole. Because sound travels at different speeds through soil, rock, and fossil remains, the waves are distorted between their source and the microphones. A computer analyzes the vibrations sensed by the mikes and reconstructs an image of the ground traversed by the waves.

Using this technology, scientists were able to confirm that seismosaurus, as the newly discovered beast was dubbed (the name means "earthshaker"), was at least 120 feet long. By plotting the location of the bones, they could draw conclusions about the conditions of its death and design precise plans for subsequent digging.

The device used to shake the ground was ideal for hunting giant reptiles: It fired soft-metal eight-gauge slugs into the ground, where they kicked off sound waves. In effect, the scientists were stalking this giant among dinosaurs with a simple shotgun. ☐

As sound vibrations from a shotgun blast *(far left)* ripple outward, their velocity is altered by density differences in the rock along their subterranean path. A tier of sensitive microphones *(below)* feeds the phase—or angle—and arrival time of the vibrations to a computer *(inset),* which calculates the location of the mineralized remains of a fossil dinosaur.

Emerald Isles

The vast tropical rain forests that girdle earth's equator are disappearing at the rate of seventy acres per minute, burned or cut to produce lumber, farmland, and pastures. But these lush jungles are more than land and stands of timber. Beneath the thick canopy of leaves, millions of interdependent species coexist—at least half of the world's species are crammed into an area comprising only about six percent of the planet's surface.

While politicians and diplomats juggle the complex social and economic issues of conservation and land use, tropical biologists have been racing to document and perhaps save some of these species, most still uncatalogued. The degree of species diversity is mind-boggling. One researcher found a single tree in Peru harboring forty-six species of ants, as many as inhabit the British Isles. A thirty-acre forest sample in Indonesia was found to support more than 700 tree species, about the number occurring in the entire continent of North America.

All this genetic richness is intertwined with ecological bargains of baffling complexity. Trees produce favorite foods for the animals that transport their pollen and seeds, or they offer shelter to ants that roam the branches, cleaning away the encroaching seeds of parasites. To defend themselves against legions of destructive insects, many plants have evolved poisonous substances that only the creatures in league with them can tolerate. In the jungle, the web of life is so densely drawn that when one species vanishes, it often takes others with it.

These disappearances also foreclose on human opportunity, for plants and animals can have great value as sources of food or medicine. At least 40 percent of the prescription medicine sold in the United States have ingredients drawn from natural sources, many of them native to the tropical rain forests. The fast-growing winged bean of New Guinea is edible from root to flower and possesses the nutritional value of soybeans. A single babassu palm from the Amazon basin produces a quarter-barrel of oil each year. The rosy periwinkle of Madagascar contains two alkaloids that are effective against some cancers. Nearly every cultivated food plant has a wild tropical cousin, a supply of genes that, added to domesticated breeds, could greatly increase the yield and resilience of some key crops. Despite a long and growing list of candidates for human use, however, the real potential has barely been tapped—and time may be running out.

In fact, no one really knows how long the jungles can endure or how much diminution they can

Sunlight filters through the high canopy of a Costa Rican rain forest, bringing life to a tangle of liana vines and tree-living plants, home to an incredible diversity of species.

stand before they, and their unassessed cornucopia of benefits, vanish altogether. To find out, naturalists have joined in the cutting.

An experiment devised in 1976 by Smithsonian Institution biologist Thomas Lovejoy involves creating cut patches of Brazilian rain forest to form islands of trees, then studying each tract to see how its plants and animals fare. The islands range in size from about 2 to 25,000 acres and are in a sense sacrificial. As the isolated patches of forest gradually deteriorate, project scientists note which species leave or die off, and in what order. Ultimately, the program should demonstrate how small a wilderness preserve can be while still maintaining its naturally wild character.

Lovejoy's project has already produced some partial answers. In the smallest plots, the bird population more than doubled soon after an island became isolated, as refugees flew in from the deforested zone. But after about six months, there was an abrupt decline. Apparently, the crowding of birds overtaxed an already limited food supply, and competition drove the numbers down. Some avian species found themselves without important allies. The woodcreepers, for example, rely entirely on army ants to flush out such prey as grasshoppers and cockroaches. But army ants, which cover as much as 60 acres in their periodic forays, could not survive in the smaller areas. They vanished, and the woodcreepers vanished with them.

Larger, 25-acre islands turned out to be too small to support large mammals, such as the piglike peccaries. Their departure left no animals to create wallows with standing water, and so three species of frogs also disappeared.

Plants at the edges of the plots suffered from unaccustomed sunlight and wind, formerly screened out by the overarching canopy of trees. Weakened by their exposure, they quickly gave ground to shorter second-growth plants that flourish when the surrounding forest is destroyed. In the experiment, such secondary growth overran the 2- and 25-acre islands of forest in just a few months.

Scheduled to run until at least 1999, the study does more than establish a minimum viable size for the remaining rain forests. Scientists believe that the tropical forests have naturally waxed and waned with variations in global climate. In hard times, these vast jungles shrank to green islands in seas of scrub and grass; then, as climatic conditions became favorable once more, the rain forests spread, linking the islands with great stands of trees. Thus, Lovejoy's islands of wilderness could be the forerunners of larger nuclei that would spread and join together, replenishing the clear-cut fields around them. □

A Shrinking Gene Pool

The number of plant and animal species on earth—variously estimated at 5 million to 30 million—is fast dwindling, in a mass extinction of proportions not seen since the dinosaurs died off 65 million years ago. Among contemporary birds and mammals alone, which make up only some 13,000 species in all, the last century has seen the disappearance of about one species a year.

Many biologists believe that this rate of extinction is at least a hundred times faster than it would be were human activity removed from the equation. The effects of civilization have been particularly harsh on islands, lakes, and other environments that are isolated or closely circumscribed. In Polynesia, for example, hunting and logging have eliminated about half of all the bird species.

Even as some species of plants and animals vanish, however, others are observed for the first time. To date, only about one and a half million are actually known to science—that is, they have been named and described. Unknown species crop up constantly. A study of nineteen trees in a Panamanian forest, for example, uncovered 950 species of beetles; more than three-quarters of them were previously uncatalogued.

Given this apparent biological plenty, the loss of species might seem a small problem, especially as so many seem to be minor variations on a theme, such as the Panamanian beetles. But many scientists assert the need for maximum diversity within the world's total genetic possibilities—the gene pool. These researchers fear that the accelerating rate of species extinction could reverse nature's climb toward ever greater multiplicity and diminish the overall viability of life on the planet. □

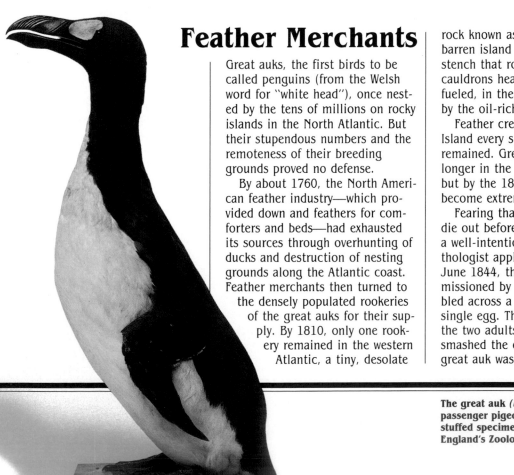

Flight of the Dodo

The dodo was a large, flightless bird discovered in 1598 by European explorers of Mauritius, its island home in the Indian Ocean. Impressed by the bird's ungainly appearance and vulnerability, its discoverers gave it the name *doudo,* Portuguese for "simpleton." The turkey-size creatures were thriving on the uninhabited volcanic isle, where they had no natural predators.

That situation changed as the island came to be a regular stopping place for ships on long passages. Sailors who had existed for months on meager rations were eager to indulge in fresh meat, even if it was tough and bitter, as was the dodo's. After the island

became a Dutch colony in 1644, extermination of the dodo was inevitable. The birds were almost tame; it was simple to walk up to them and crush their skulls with wooden clubs. Even if a dodo chose to flee, it could not outrun an able-bodied man.

While the adults died at human hands, their offspring fell prey to rats, dogs, cats, monkeys, and pigs, all introduced by the colonists and quick to adapt to the new environment. By 1680, Mauritius was entirely overrun by hu-

mans and their domestic animals; and the dodo, less than a century after it had been discovered, was gone. In fact, so swift and absolute had been its disappearance that, well into the nineteenth century, its existence was considered debatable, like the unicorn's. Only after a Mauritius resident presented scientists with several skeletons in 1865 was the dodo's existence confirmed. □

Feather Merchants

Great auks, the first birds to be called penguins (from the Welsh word for "white head"), once nested by the tens of millions on rocky islands in the North Atlantic. But their stupendous numbers and the remoteness of their breeding grounds proved no defense.

By about 1760, the North American feather industry—which provided down and feathers for comforters and beds—had exhausted its sources through overhunting of ducks and destruction of nesting grounds along the Atlantic coast. Feather merchants then turned to the densely populated rookeries of the great auks for their supply. By 1810, only one rookery remained in the western Atlantic, a tiny, desolate

rock known as Funk Island. The barren island was named for the stench that rose from defeathering cauldrons heated by fires that were fueled, in the absence of firewood, by the oil-rich bodies of birds.

Feather crews returned to Funk Island every spring until no birds remained. Great auks lasted a little longer in the vicinity of Iceland, but by the 1840s, these also had become extremely rare.

Fearing that the species would die out before it had been studied, a well-intentioned Icelandic ornithologist applied the final blow. In June 1844, three fishermen, commissioned by the collector, stumbled across a breeding pair with a single egg. They pursued and killed the two adults with clubs and smashed the egg in the chase. The great auk was never seen again. □

The great auk *(left)*, dodo *(above)*, and passenger pigeon *(right)* survive only as stuffed specimens such as these from England's Zoological Museum at Tring.

GREAT AUK,

Passing Pigeons

Martha, the last of the passenger pigeons, died in the Cincinnati Zoo on September 1, 1914, in a cage she shared with a handful of mourning doves. Had she lived only half a century earlier, she might have been part of a flock that passed over Cincinnati—two billion strong, a mile wide, and 320 miles long.

Flocks of that size were a routine sight in the passenger pigeon's heyday. For three days in 1813, the pioneering ornithologist John James Audubon observed columns of the birds so dense that the "light of the noonday sun was obscured as by an eclipse." Visiting their nesting sites, Audubon found vast areas where tree limbs had been shattered by the weight of roosting birds.

Such concentrations spelled disaster for the passenger pigeons, so called because they seemed always to be on the move. Hunted as a source of meat,

their numbers had already begun to dwindle along the eastern seaboard much earlier, by the 1770s. Hunters knocked young birds from their nests with poles and used "stool pigeons"—tethered birds with their eyes sewn shut, and now a slang term for informers—to lure others within range of nets. The advent of railroads and loss of habitat sealed the fate of the swift-flying birds. Now, no nesting ground was out of reach of the hunters, who also had a convenient way of shipping their prey to urban markets. By 1878, there were only about 50 million passenger pigeons remaining.

In the next two decades, every major nesting colony was either destroyed or disrupted by hunters. Prevented from breeding, the pigeons were unable to replenish their numbers, and the population plummeted as older birds died. Zoo breeding programs proved unsuccessful, and when the last of the wild passenger pigeons was killed in Ohio in 1900, their extinction became inevitable. By the spring of 1909, only three pigeons remained in the Cincinnati Zoo. By the end of 1910, there was only Martha, who lived to the remarkable age of twenty-nine. Her death in 1914 was witnessed only by her keeper and his son; she received a short notice in the *Cincinnati Enquirer.* □

Succulent Sea Cows

The shipwrecked crewmen of Danish explorer Vitus J. Bering's last arctic expedition were near the end of their tether in 1741 when they first saw what some reckoned to be mermaids. Already marooned for the long northern winter on a jagged island, the homesick sailors fell easily into fantasy at the sight of grayish-pink animals with milk-filled breasts, swimming in the distance. At closer hand, however, wishful thinking gave way to the massive reality of thirty-foot, seven-ton mammals. They came to be known as Steller's sea cows, named for Georg Steller, the expedition's German physician—and the only naturalist ever to see these remarkable creatures alive.

The sea cows, now believed to have descended from a land mammal that was also ancestral to elephants, could swim like seals but also used their stumplike forelimbs to crawl along the bottom. They grazed on seaweed growing in shallow water, tearing it up like horses pawing the ground. Unfortunately, their feeding habits brought them within easy range of the hungry sailors' harpoons.

The famished seamen speared a sea cow and dragged it ashore, where they slaughtered it. They found the red meat delicious, with the curious property of doubling in size when cooked. The fat could be rendered into a clear fluid that tasted like sweet almond oil and burned with a smokeless, odor-free flame. The great beasts were too tasty for their own good.

Bering's crew (their captain died on the desolate island that later ◊

bore his name) eventually built a small vessel and made their way home, bearing news of the prodigious new food source they had discovered in the arctic wastes. Soon other ships returned to the same waters to harvest the pelts of sea otters and to provision their ships with meat. It was a wasteful practice. One Steller's sea cow could feed thirty-three men for a month; but, for every one that was actually beached for the kill, another four were critically wounded and abandoned to the sea. So wanton was the slaughter that the entire Steller's sea cow population was extinguished by 1767—just twenty-five years after their discovery by Europeans. □

Staving Off Extinctions

Noah, a rare Indian desert cat, was one of the heroes of the fight against extinction. Born on February 7, 1989, he marked the culmination of years of research and trials at the Center for Reproduction of Endangered Wildlife, or CREW, at the Cincinnati Zoo. Because exotic cats are often reluctant to mate in captivity, CREW had attempted to develop an alternative way of propagating the vanishing race of wild felines, and Noah was a promising result. Combining eggs collected from a female Indian desert cat with sperm from a male, CREW specialists produced an embryo that was then implanted in Noah's surrogate mother: a common domestic cat.

Born after an otherwise routine pregnancy, Noah died three months later of a viral infection unrelated to his extraordinary beginnings. But he had blazed a trail for his fellows. The technique used to create Noah now promises to help replenish populations of small exotic cats threatened by the shrinking of their natural habitats. It also offers the benefit of producing test-tube kittens from geographically separated parents, expanding the endangered species' gene pool. Some biologists even speculate about the possibility of "frozen zoos," where embryos could wait to be born until there was again a place for them to live.

Plants also benefit from such sophisticated techniques as cryopreservation, which can sustain the viability of some seeds by storing them in liquid nitrogen cooled to minus 320 degrees Fahrenheit. For tropical plants whose seeds cannot be dried or frozen, a small amount of tissue can be deep frozen and preserved.

The tissue can then be stimulated with hormones to regenerate shoots and roots.

Much of this material resides in more than two hundred seed banks in a worldwide network established by the United Nations. But, because all seeds eventually lose their vitality with age, volunteer seed savers sustain them by planting "heirloom" varieties that continue to produce new seed. One heirloom grower has 400 different kinds of squash in his garden.

Scientists are also attempting to restore entire habitats and ecosystems. On a broad, flat plot of land west of Chicago, researchers have been working with seeds of nearly extinct plants, trying to re-create a patch of the tall-grass prairie that once extended across much of the continent's midsection. Although the project requires little high technology, it is close to the heart of modern science. The prairie is surrounded by an earthen mound covering the subterranean four-mile-long ring of the Fermilab particle accelerator, one of the most complex scientific instruments ever built. □

Potatoes grown
by a farmer in the
Seed Savers Ex-
change preserve the
genetic diversity
of their kind.

Hairy-eared dwarf lemur *(Allocebus trichotis)*

Stinking corpse lily *(Rafflesia arnoldi)*

Mountain zebra *(Equus zebra)*

The Doomed

The road to extinction is so crowded that even compiling a list of threatened species becomes a major undertaking. The U.S. government publishes a conservative estimate of species that it considers endangered (in imminent danger of extinction) and threatened (likely to become endangered if nothing changes). By the year 1990, about 1,000 species had been placed on the official list.

Using less conservative measures, the Geneva-based International Union for the Conservation of Nature and Natural Resources has released a chilling list of more than 30,000 troubled species worldwide. These include not only endangered and threatened species but also those that are "rare and vulnerable" as a consequence of habitat destruction, pollution, hunting, and collecting. □

ACKNOWLEDGMENTS

The editors wish to thank these individuals and institutions for their valuable assistance:

Shirley Bachelor, U.S. Postal Service, Atlanta, Ga.; Herbert L. Belisle, Choctaw, Okla.; Knute Berger, Kirkland, Wash.; Albert Bergesen, University of Arizona, Tucson; Anne Berman, Martin's West, Baltimore, Md.; Manfred Börsch, Stadtarchiv, Hameln; Elaine Durnin Bougher, *Linn's Stamp News*, Sidney, Ohio; John Carlson, Bladensburg, Md.; Jerry C. Cashion, The Historical Society of North Carolina, Raleigh, N.C.; K. C. Chang, Peabody Museum, Harvard University, Cambridge, Mass.; Kim Cherry, Media and Communications Specialist, First Tennessee Bank, Memphis; Mario Colletti, Ministero del Tesoro, Rome; Susan Dalton, The American Film Institute, Washington, D.C.; Antonio D'Ambrosio, Soprintendenza Archeologica, Pompei; Gregory Danz, Financial Crimes Unit, Chicago Police Department, Chicago; Richard Daugherty, Lacey, Wash.; Marilyn S. Dicus, Washington Metropolitan Area Transit Authority, Washington, D.C.; Hamilton Dix, U.S. Mint, Office of Public Affairs, Washington, D.C.; Betsy L. Dresser, Center for Reproduction of Endangered Wildlife, Cincinnati Zoo, Cincinnati, Ohio; Louis Eberhardt, U.S. Postal Service, Washington, D.C.; Giuseppe Foglia, Naples; David Freidel, Southern Methodist University, Dallas, Tex.; Frances E. Gardner, U.S. Postal Service, Washington, D.C.; Klaus Goldmann, Staatliche Museen Preussischer Kulturbesitz, Museum für Vor-und Frühgeschichte, West Berlin; James Grantham, Spartanburg Animal Clinic, Spartanburg, S.C.; Chris Haws, WGBH Educational Foundation, Boston, Mass.; Greg Hawthorne, Main Post Office, St. Paul, Minn.; Ken Holum, Department of History, University of Maryland, College Park; Robert Howley, Seabrook, N.H.; Frances Jones, Counselor Affairs Office, State Department, Washington, D.C.; Rick Jones, METRO Lost and Found, Washington, D.C.; Ruth Kirk, Tacoma, Wash.; Jürgen Küster, Deutsches Post Museum, Frankfurt; Elgen and Marie Long, San Mateo, Calif.; Walter von Lukadow, Auskunftsstelle für Parapsychologie, Freiburg; Gordon McEwan, Dumbarton Oaks, Washington, D.C.; Paul S. Martin, Department of Geosciences, University of Arizona, Tucson; Bernhard Meier, Grevenbrück; Frederick G. Meyer, U.S. National Arboretum, Washington, D.C.; Dennis Murphy, New Castle, N.H.; Antonio Nazzaro, Osservatorio Vesuviano, Naples; Ivor Noël Hume, Williamsburg, Va.; Keeley Parker, Macah Museum, Neah Bay, Wash.; Ann Renker, Macah Museum, Neah Bay, Wash.; Giovanni Ricciardi, Osservatorio Vesuviano, Naples; Claudio Ripa, Naples; Grant Roehmer, Rochester, N.Y.; Christiane Roger, Société Francaise de Photographie, Paris; Raymond Rye, Department of Paleobiology, Smithsonian Institution, Washington, D.C.; Luigi Scattolon, Rome;, Linda Schele, Department of Art—Art History, University of Texas, Austin; Jack Sciacca, MTA Lost and Found, Brooklyn, N.Y.; Hershel Shanks, Washington, D.C.; Cecilia Smith, U.S. Postal Service, New York; Merily Smith, Library of Congress, Washington, D.C.; Andrew J. Sozzi, New York Division of the U.S. Postal Service, New York; Paul Spehr, Archivist, Library of Congress, Washington, D.C.; Steven M. Stanley, Department of Earth and Planetary Science, Johns Hopkins University, Baltimore, Md.; Vickie Stidham, Center for Reproduction of Endangered Wildlife, Cincinnati Zoo, Cincinnati, Ohio; Randall L. Susman, Department of Anatomical Sciences, State University of New York, Stony Brook, N.Y.; Erik Trinkaus, Department of Anthropology, University of New Mexico, Albuquerque; Alan Walker, Department of Cell Biology and Anatomy, Johns Hopkins School of Medicine, Baltimore, Md.; Alan Witten, Oak Ridge National Laboratory, Oak Ridge, Tenn.

PICTURE CREDITS

The sources for the illustrations that appear in this book are listed below. Credits from left to right are separated by semicolons, from top to bottom by dashes.

Cover: Larry Burrows for *LIFE,* background, © Gill C. Kenny/The Image Bank, New York. **3:** Larry Burrows for *LIFE.* **7:** From the *The Howitzer,* United States Military Academy, West Point Yearbook, 1949, background, Craig Arness/Westlight. **8, 9:** Loren McIntyre—from *Exploration Fawcett,* by Lieutenant Colonel P. H. Fawcett, Hutchinson, London, 1953. **10:** Dr. Owen Beattie, University of Alberta. **11:** Scott Polar Research Institute, Cambridge; National Maritime Museum, Greenwich (2), B/W print hand colored by Karen Doyle. **12, 13:** Mitchell Library, State Library of New South Wales, Australia. **14, 15:** Hebridean Press Service, W. G. Lucas. **16:** Peabody Museum of Salem, Salem, Massachusetts. **17:** Culver Pictures, Inc., New York, hand colored by Karen Doyle. **19:** AP/Wide World Photos, New York; from *Around the World in the Sloop Spray,* by Captain Joshua Slocum, Charles Scribner's Sons, New York, 1903, hand colored by Karen Doyle. **20:** The Hulton Picture Company, London. **21:** Fil Hunter. **22:** Fil Hunter, background, courtesy Craig Arness/Westlight. **23:** Library of Congress no. 4755-LC-US26220182, hand colored by Karen Doyle—UPI/Bettmann, New York. **24:** Katherine Wetzel, courtesy Lifesaving Museum of Virginia Beach; Maine Maritime Museum, Bath. **25:** AP/Wide World Photos, New York. **26:** Culver Pictures, Inc. **27:** Alex Stewart/The Image Bank, New York; Royal Geographical Society, London. **28:** UPI/Bettman, New York. **29:** Popperfoto, London. **30, 31:** Artwork by Time-Life Books. **32:** AP/Wide World Photos, New York. **33:** Courtesy Time Inc. Magazines Picture Collection. **34, 35:** National Archives, neg. no. 242-hb-48400-530; from *The Howitzer,* United States Military Academy, West Point Yearbook, 1949. **36:** Popperfoto, London. **37:** Film Study Center, Harvard University. **38:** Photograph by Bob Salmon, *The Sunday Times,* London. **39:** Keystone, New York. **40:** Times Newspapers Ltd., London. **41:** AP/Wide World Photos, New York—courtesy Time Inc. Magazines Picture Collection. **42:** Topham Picture Source, Edenbridge, Kent; Camera Press Ltd., London. **43:** Fred Ward/Black Star, New York. **44:** © Brian Drake/Photo Researchers, Inc., New York. **45:** Fil Hunter, inset, photograph by Cynthia Johnson. **46:** Apolinar Gallardo. **47:** David Jeffrey/The Image Bank, New York, inset, Fil Hunter. **48:** Erwin Bohm, Mainz, courtesy Deutsches Postmuseum, Frankfurt. **49:** Postmark Collectors Club Museum, Republic, Ohio; Library of Congress no. LC-US-26238267. **50:** Adam Bartos—AP/Wide World Photos, New York. **51:** Antonio Scattolon, Rome—David Jeffrey/The Image Bank, New York. **52:** AP/Wide World Photos, New York; Fil Hunter. **53:** Spartanburg Animal Clinic, Spartanburg, South Carolina, courtesy Dr. James Grantham—Renée Comet. **54:** Fil Hunter. **55:** Photofest, New York—Scala, Florence, courtesy Archivio di Stato, Siena. **57:** From *Paul Daniels and the Story of Magic,* by John Fisher, Jonathan Cape, London, 1987, © John Fisher, background, © William James Warren/Westlight. **58:** Artwork by Time-Life Books—Giraudon, Paris. **59:** Courtesy Robert Lund, American Museum of Magic, Marshall, Michigan. **60, 61:** Fil Hunter. **62:** Mary Evans Picture Library, London, hand colored by Karen Doyle. **64:** © The Edwin A. Dawes Collection, Hull, Yorkshire. **66:** From *Paul Daniels and the Story of*

BIBLIOGRAPHY

Books

Academic American Encyclopedia. Princeton, N.J.: Aretê, 1980.

Andrews, Val. *A Gift from the Gods: The Story of Chung Ling Soo Marvellous Chinese Conjurer.* Warwickshire: Goodliffe, 1981.

Beattie, Owen, and John Geiger. *Frozen in Time: Unlocking the Secrets of the Franklin Expedition.* Saskatoon, Saskatchewan: Western Producer Prairie Books, 1988.

Begg, Paul. *Into Thin Air: People Who Disappear.* London: David & Charles, 1979.

Bierman, John. *Righteous Gentile: The Story of Raoul Wallenberg, Missing Hero of the Holocaust.* New York: Viking Press, 1981.

Bowyer, J. Barton. *Cheating.* New York: St. Martin's Press, 1980.

Brion, Marcel. *Pompeii and Herculaneum: The Glory and the Grief.* Translated by John Rosenberg. New York: Crown, 1960.

The Cambridge Encyclopedia of Earth Sciences. Edited by David G. Smith. Cambridge: Cambridge University Press, 1981.

Canning, John (Ed.). *Fifty True Mysteries of the Sea.* New York: Dorset Press, 1988.

Chang, Kwang-chih:
The Archaeology of Ancient China (4th ed.). New Haven: Yale University Press, 1986.
Shang Civilization. New Haven: Yale University Press, 1980.

Chisholm, Alec H. *Strange Journey: The Adventures of Ludwig Leichhardt and John Gilbert.* Adelaide, Australia: Rigby Limited, 1973.

Christopher, Milbourne:

Houdini: A Pictorial Life. New York: Thomas Y. Crowell, 1976.
The Illustrated History of Magic. New York: Thomas Y. Crowell, 1973.
Panorama of Magic. New York: Dover Publications, 1962.

Churchill, Allen. *They Never Came Back.* Garden City, N.Y.: Doubleday, 1960.

Ciochon, Russell L., and Robert S. Corruccini (Eds.). *New Interpretations of Ape and Human Ancestry.* New York: Plenum Press, 1983.

Claflin, Edward, and Jeff Sheridan. *Street Magic: An Illustrated History of Wandering Magicians and Their Conjuring Arts.* Garden City, N.Y.: Dolphin Books, 1977.

Clapp, Jane. *Vanishing Point.* New York: Scarecrow Press, 1961.

Clark, David. *Victor Grayson: Labour's Lost Leader.* London: Quartet Books, 1985.

Clayton, Peter A., and Martin J. Price. *The Seven Wonders of the Ancient World.* London: Routledge, 1988.

Coe, Michael D.:
The Maya (4th ed.). London: Thames & Hudson, 1987.
Mexico (3d ed.). London: Thames & Hudson, 1984.

Coe, Michael D., Dean Snow, and Elizabeth Benson. *Atlas of Ancient America.* New York: Facts on File Publications, 1986.

Cœdès, George. *Angkor.* Edited and translated by Emily Floyd Gardiner. Hong Kong: Oxford University Press, 1963.

Cohen, Daniel:
The Encyclopedia of Unsolved Crimes. New

York: Dodd, Mead, 1988.
The Encyclopedia of the Strange. New York: Avon, 1985.

Collier's Encyclopedia (Vol. 5). New York: Macmillan, 1982.

Columbia Encyclopedia. New York: Columbia University Press, 1979.

Constable, George, and the Editors of Time-Life Books. *The Neanderthals* (The Emergence of Man series). New York: Time-Life Books, 1973.

Crater, Stella, and Oscar Fraley. *The Empty Robe.* Garden City, N.Y.: Doubleday, 1961.

Culbert, T. Patrick (Ed.). *The Classic Maya Collapse.* Albuquerque: University of New Mexico Press, 1973.

Culbert, T. Patrick. *The Lost Civilization: The Story of the Classic Maya.* New York: Harper & Row, 1974.

Dawes, Edwin A. *The Great Illusionists.* Secaucus, N.J.: Chartwell Books, 1979.

Day, David. *Vanished Species* (rev. ed.). New York: Gallery Books, 1989.

Desfor, Irving. *Great Magicians in Great Moments.* Pomeroy, Ohio: Lee Jacobs Productions, 1983.

Dexter, Will (William Thomas Pritchard). *This is Magic: Secrets of the Conjurer's Craft.* New York: Citadel Press, 1958.

Donaldson, Norman, and Betty Donaldson. *How Did They Die?* New York: St. Martin's Press, 1980.

Dumbarton Oaks Conference on the Olmec, October 28th and 29th, 1967. Edited by Elizabeth P. Benson. Washington, D.C.: Dumbarton Oaks Research Library & Collection Trustees for Harvard University, 1968.

Eldredge, Niles, and Steven M. Stanley (Eds.). *Living Fossils.* New York: Springer Verlag, 1984.

Empires Besieged (The TimeFrame series). Alexandria, Va.: Time-Life Books, 1988.

The Encyclopedia Americana (Vols. 5 & 21). Danbury, Conn.: Grolier, 1986.

Encyclopædia Britannica (Vol. 4). Chicago: Encyclopædia Britannica, 1960.

Encyclopaedia Judaica (Vol. 15). Jerusalem: Keter Publishing House, 1973.

Fawcett, Percy Harrison. *Exploration Fawcett.* London: Hutchinson, 1953.

The First Men (The Emergence of Man series). New York: Time-Life Books, 1973.

Fischer, Ottokar. *Illustrated Magic.* Toronto: Coles, 1980.

Fisher, David. *The War Magician.* New York: Coward-McCann, 1983.

Fisher, John. *Paul Daniels and the Story of Magic.* London: Jonathan Cape, 1987.

Fleming, Peter. *Brazilian Adventure.* New York, Charles Scribner's Sons, 1960.

Flemming, Nicholas C. *Cities in the Sea.* Garden City, N.Y.: Doubleday, 1971.

Forrest, John. *Explorations in Australia.* New York: Greenwood Press, 1969 (reprint of 1875 edition).

Fort, Charles. *The Complete Books of Charles Fort.* New York: Dover Publications, 1974.

Fraser, Ronald. *In Hiding: The Life of Manuel Cortes.* New York: Pantheon Books, 1972.

Freeman, Roger A. *Camouflage & Markings.* London: Ducimus Books, 1974.

Fuller, Errol. *Extinct Birds.* New York: Facts on File Publications, 1987.

Furneaux, Rupert. *The World's Most Intriguing True Mysteries.* New York: Arco, 1966.

Gibson, Walter. *Secrets of Magic: Ancient and Modern.* New York: Grosset & Dunlap, 1967.

Goerner, Fred. *The Search for Amelia Earhart.* Garden City, N.Y.: Doubleday, 1966.

Grine, F. E. (Ed.). Hawthorne, N.Y.: Aldine de Gruyter, 1988.

Gunning, Thomas G. *Strange Mysteries.* New York: Dodd, Mead, 1987.

Hall, John. *Four Famous Mysteries.* London: Nisbet, 1922.

Halstead, L. B. *The Search for the Past.* Garden City, N.Y.: Doubleday, 1982.

Hamblin, Dora Jane, and the Editors of Time-Life Books. *The Etruscans* (The Emergence of Man series). New York: Time-Life Books, 1975.

Hartcup, Guy. *Camouflage: A History of Concealment and Deception in War.* New York: Charles Scribner's Sons, 1980.

Hayman, LeRoy. *Thirteen Who Vanished: True Stories of Mysterious Disappearances.* New York: Julian Messner, 1979.

Henning, Doug, and Charles Reynolds. *Houdini: His Legend and His Magic.* New York: Times Books, 1977.

Hitching, Francis. *The World Atlas of Mysteries.* London: William Collins Sons, 1978.

Holum, Kenneth G., et al. *King Herod's Dream: Caesarea on the Sea.* New York: W. W. Norton, 1988.

Holzel, Tom, and Audrey Salkeld. *First on Everest: The Mystery of Mallory and Irvine.* New York: Henry Holt, 1986.

Hopkins, Albert A. (Ed. and comp.). *Magic: Stage Illusions and Scientific Diversions.* New York: Arno Press, 1977.

Kaufman, Les, and Kenneth Mallory (Eds.). *The Last Extinction.* Cambridge, Mass.: MIT Press, 1986.

Kirk, Ruth, and Richard D. Daugherty. *Hunters of the Whale.* New York: William Morrow, 1974.

Klaas, Joe. *Amelia Earhart Lives: A Trip through Intrigue to Find America's First Lady of Mystery.* New York: McGraw-Hill, 1970.

Kraus, Theodor. *Pompeii and Herculaneum: The Living Cities of the Dead.* Translated by Robert Erich Wolf. New York: Harry N. Abrams, 1975.

Lehane, Brendan, and the Editors of Time-Life Books. *The Northwest Passage.* (The Seafarers series). Alexandria, Va.: Time-Life Books, 1981.

Lewin, Roger. *Thread of Life.* Washington, D.C.: Smithsonian Books, 1982.

Li Chi. *Anyang.* Seattle: University of Washington Press, 1977.

Lovejoy, Thomas E., et al. "Ecosystem Decay of Amazon Forest Remnants." In *Extinctions,* edited by Matthew H. Nitecki. Chicago: University of Chicago Press, 1984.

Lovell, Mary S. *The Sound of Wings: The Life of Amelia Earhart.* New York: St. Martin's Press, 1989.

McClement, Fred. *The Strange Case of Ambrose Small.* Toronto: McClelland & Stewart, 1974.

Machlin, Milt. *The Search for Michael Rockefeller.* New York: G. P. Putnam's Sons, 1972.

Maddocks, Melvin, and the Editors of Time-Life Books. *The Great Liners* (The Seafarers series). Alexandria, Va.: Time-Life Books, 1978.

Making Today's Books Last. Washington, D.C.: Library of Congress, 1985.

Marnham, Patrick. *Trail of Havoc: In the Steps of Lord Lucan.* London: Penguin Books, 1988.

Martin, Paul S., and Richard G. Klein (Eds.). *Quaternary Extinctions: A Prehistoric Revolution.* Tucson, Ariz.: University of Arizona Press, 1984.

Maskelyne, Jasper. *Magic—Top Secret.* London: Stanley Paul, 1949.

Moolman, Valerie, and the Editors of Time-Life Books. *Women Aloft* (The Epic of Flight series). Alexandria, Va.: Time-Life Books, 1981.

Mysteries of the Unexplained. Pleasantville, N.Y.: Reader's Digest Association, 1982.

Nash, Jay Robert. *Among the Missing: An Anecdotal History of Missing Persons from 1800 to the Present.* New York: Simon & Schuster, 1978.

Newby, Eric. *The Rand McNally Atlas of Exploration.* New York: Rand McNally, 1975.

The New Encyclopædia Britannica (Vol. 2, 15th ed.). Chicago: Encylopædia Britannica, 1984.

Nicholson, Christopher. *Rock Lighthouses of Britain.* Cambridge: Patrick Stephens, 1983.

Noël Hume, Ivor. *Martin's Hundred.* New York: Alfred A. Knopf, 1982.

O'Connor, Richard. *Ambrose Bierce: A Biography.* Boston: Little, Brown, 1967.

O'Donnell, Elliott. *Strange Disappearances.* New Hyde Park, N.Y.: University Books, 1972.

Oldfield, Margery L. *The Value of Conserving Genetic Resources.* Washington, D.C.: U.S. Department of the Interior, 1984.

Ommanney, F. D., and the Editors of Time-Life Books. *The Fishes.* (The Life Nature Library series, rev. ed.). Alexandria, Va.: Time-Life Books, 1980.

Out of This World: The Illustrated Library of the Bizarre and Extraordinary. New York: Phoebus Publishing, 1978.

Page, Denys L. *History and the Homeric Iliad.* Berkeley: University of California Press, 1959.

Pugh, Marshall. *Commander Crabb.* London: Macmillan, 1956.

Reit, Seymour. *Masquerade.* New York: Hawthorn Books, 1978.

Reptiles & Amphibians (The Wild, Wild World of Animals series). New York: Time-Life Films, 1976.

Rich, Doris L. *Amelia Earhart: A Biography.* Washington, D.C.: Smithsonian Institution Press, 1989.

Sabloff, Jeremy A. (Ed.). *Archaeology* (Vol. 1 of *Supplement to the Handbook of Middle American Indians,* edited by Victoria Reifler Bricker). Austin: University of Texas Press, 1981.

Sanders, Ronald. *Lost Tribes and Promised Lands.* Boston: Little, Brown, 1978.

Schele, Linda, and David Freidel. *A Forest of Kings: The Untold Story of the Ancient Maya.* New York: William Morrow, 1990.

Service, Alastair. *Lost Worlds.* New York: Arco Publishing, 1981.

Shanks, Hershel. *Judaism in Stone: The Archaeology of Ancient Synagogues.* New York:

Harper & Row and Biblical Archaeology Society, 1979.

Shapiro, Harry L. *Peking Man.* New York: Simon & Schuster, 1974.

Sheridan, Walter. *The Fall and Rise of Jimmy Hoffa.* New York: Saturday Review Press, 1972.

Slocum, Victor. *Capt. Joshua Slocum: The Life and Voyages of America's Best Known Sailor* (rev. ed.). White Plains, N.Y.: Sheridan House, 1981.

Stanley, Steven M.:

Extinction. New York: Scientific American Books, 1987.

"Marine Mass Extinctions: A Dominant Role for Temperature." In *Extinctions,* edited by Matthew H. Nitecki. Chicago: University of Chicago Press, 1984.

Stick, David. *Graveyard of the Atlantic: Shipwrecks of the North Carolina Coast.* Chapel Hill, N.C.: University of North Carolina Press, 1952.

Sweetman, Bill. *Stealth Aircraft.* Osceola, Wis.: Motorbooks, 1986.

Teller, Walter Magnes:

Joshua Slocum. New Brunswick: Rutgers University Press, 1971.

The Voyages of Joshua Slocum. New Brunswick: Rutgers University Press, 1958.

Thorndike, Joseph J., Jr. (Ed.). *Mysteries of the Deep.* New York: American Heritage, 1980.

Tomalin, Nicholas, and Ron Hall. *The Strange Last Voyage of Donald Crowhurst.* New York: Stein & Day, 1970.

Trinkaus, Erik. *The Shanidar Neandertals.* New York: Academic Press, 1983.

Wallechinsky, David, and Irving Wallace. *The People's Almanac.* Garden City, N.Y.: Doubleday, 1975.

Warren, William. *The Legendary American: The Remarkable Career and Strange Disappearance of Jim Thompson.* Boston: Houghton Mifflin, 1970.

Westwood, Jennifer (Ed.). *The Atlas of Mysterious Places.* New York: Weidenfeld & Nicolson, 1987.

Wiggins, Robert A. *Ambrose Bierce.* Minneapolis: University of Minnesota Press, 1964.

Wilson, Colin, and Damon Wilson. *The Encyclopedia of Unsolved Mysteries.* Chicago: Contemporary Books, 1988.

Wilson, Colin: *Enigmas and Mysteries.* Garden City, N.Y.: Doubleday, 1976.

The World Almanac and Book of Facts 1990. New York: World Almanac, 1990.

Wright, Lawrence. *Clockwork Man.* New York: Horizon Press, 1968.

Yad Vashem Studies (Vol. 15). Edited by Livia Rothkirchen. Jerusalem: Yad Vashem, 1983.

Yoffee, Norman, and George L. Cowgill (Eds.). *The Collapse of Ancient States and Civilizations.* Tucson: University of Arizona Press, 1988.

Periodicals

Alvarez, Luis W. "Mass Extinctions Caused by Large Bolide Impacts." *Physics Today,* July 1987.

Anderson, Jack, and Dale Van Atta. "The Search for Raoul Wallenberg Goes On." *Washington Post,* December 10, 1989.

Anson, Robert Sam. "Mystery of the Thai Silk King." *Life,* May 1984.

Arnold, David. "The Mystery at the Top of Mt. Everest." *Boston Globe,* March 24, 1986.

Ashley, S., and C. P. Gilmore. "Finally: Stealth!" *Popular Science,* July 1988.

Beardsley, Tim. "B-2 or Not B-2: Stealth Bomber is the Target in a Debate on Nuclear Strategy." *Scientific American,* August 1988.

Begg, Paul. "Philadelphia Experiment: Mystery of the Vanishing Ship." *The Unexplained Mysteries of Mind Space & Time,* 1981, Vol. 5, no. 60.

Begley, Sharon, and Fiona Gleizes. "My Granddad, Neanderthal?" *Newsweek,* October 16, 1989.

Bering-Jensen, Helle. "New Clue to the Lost Colony's Fate." *Insight,* January 8, 1990.

Brain, C. K., et al. "New Evidence of Early Hominids, Their Culture and Environment from the Swartkrans Cave, South Africa." *South African Journal of Science,* October 1988.

Brean, Herbert, and Luther Conant. "The Mystery of the Missing Cadet." *Life,* April 14, 1952.

Browne, Malcolm W. "It Has Been Ballyhooed as Invisible and Unstoppable, but Critics Charge the B-2 Is a Costly Boondoggle." *New York Times Magazine,* July 17, 1988.

"B-2 to Be Delivered to Whiteman in Fiscal 1991." *Aviation Week & Space Technology,* December 5, 1988.

"Clues Are Sought on Lost American." *New York Times,* April 29, 1967.

Cohn, Jeffrey P. "Modern-Day Noahs." *Zoogoer,* March/April 1989.

Diamond, Jared. "How to Speak Neanderthal." *Discover,* January 1990.

"The Disadvantage of Extinction." *The Economist,* January 6, 1990.

Dyott, G. M. "The Search for Colonel Fawcett." *The Geographical Journal,* December 1929.

Elmer-DeWitt, Phillip. "A Bold Raid on Computer Security." *Time,* May 2, 1988.

Epstein, Nadine. "Illuminating the Maya's Path in Belize." *Smithsonian,* December 1989.

Fagan, Brian. "Readers in Maya." *Archaeology,* July/August 1989.

Fox, James:

"Is This What Happened to 'Lucky' Lucan?" *You,* October 28, 1984.

"The Luck of the Lucans." *Sunday Times,* June 6, 1975.

Grayson, Donald K. "The First Americans: Death by Natural Causes." *Natural History,* May 1987.

Grove, Noel. "Quietly Conserving Nature." *National Geographic,* December 1988.

Greenway, H. D. S. "Thailand to Close Case of Missing American." *Washington Post,* March 26, 1974.

Harvard, Andrew. "62-Year-Old Mystery of Mt. Everest." *Los Angeles Times,* August 31, 1986.

Hillman, Rolfe L., Jr. "Ambrose Bierce: He Went to War and to the Devil." *Army,* July 1974.

"The Hit on Jimmy Hoffa: The Most Notorious, Unsolved Crime of the Seventies, Explained." *Playboy,* November 1989.

Jones, Mervyn. "The Vanishing MP—a Mystery Unsolved for 55 Years." *Sunday Times Magazine,* July 13, 1975.

Karr, Lawrence F. "Film Preservation: Why Nitrate Won't Wait." *I.A.T.S.E. Official Bulletin,* Summer 1972.

Kerr, Richard A.:

"Asteroid Impact Gets More Support." *Science,* May 8, 1987.

"Huge Impact Is Favored K-T Boundary Killer." *Science,* November 11, 1988.

Kotz, Nick. "Shedding Light on Stealth." *Harper's,* August 1988.

Lamar, Jacob V. "Will This Bird Fly?" *Time,* December 5, 1988.

Lester, Elenore, and Frederick E. Werbell. "The Lost Hero of the Holocaust." *New York Times Magazine,* March 30, 1980.

Lewis, Thomas A. "How Did the Giants Die?" *International Wildlife,* September 1987.

Mahoney, Tom. "The End of Ambrose Bierce." *Esquire,* February 1936.

Marinatos, Spyridon. "Thera: Key to the Riddle of Minos." *National Geographic,* May 1972.

Martin, Paul S. "Clovisia the Beautiful!" *Natural History,* October 1987.

Marton, Kati. "The Wallenberg Mystery." *The Atlantic,* November 1980.

"More Ships Added to Mystery List." *New York Times,* June 22, 1921.

Morganthau, Tom, John Barry, and Douglas Waller. "An $80 Billion Bust?" *Newsweek,* December 5, 1988.

Morrocco, John D.:

"Air Force Unveils Design of Northrop B-2 Bomber." *Aviation Week & Space Technology,* April 25, 1988.

"USAF Unveils Stealth Fighter; Black Weapons Probe Likely." *Aviation Week & Space Technology,* November 14, 1988.

Nelson, Dale. "Deacidification at LC." *Wilson Library Bulletin,* November 1984.

Noël Hume, Ivor:
"First Look at a Lost Virginia Settlement." *National Geographic*, June 1979.
"New Clues to an Old Mystery." *National Geographic*, January 1982.
Oldfield, Margery L., and Janis B. Alcorn. "Conservation of Traditional Agroecosystems." *Bio Science*, March 1987.
Omang, Joanne. "The Hands-On Level of Deforestation." *Smithsonian*, March 1987.
"Piracy Suspected in Disappearance of 3 American Ships." *New York Times*, June 21, 1921.
Rensberger, Boyce. "Acid Test: Stalling Self-Destruction in the Stacks." *Washington Post*, August 29, 1988.
Revkin, Andrew C. "Missing: The Curious Case of Vladimir Alexandrov." *Science Digest*, July 1986.
Scott, William B. "New Design, Production Tools Will Play Key Role in B-2 Cost." *Aviation Week & Space Technology*, December 5, 1988.
Sedge, Michael H. "Sunken City of Baiae." *Oceans*, November/December 1983.
Shell, Ellen Ruppel. "Seed Banks—A Growing Concern." *Smithsonian*, January 1990.
Shipman, Pat. "The Gripping Story of Paranthropus." *Discover*, April 1989.
"Skipper's Daughter Holds Pirate Theory." *New York Times*, June 23, 1921.

Susman, Randall L.:
"Hand of *Paranthropus robustus* from Member 1, Swartkrans: Fossil Evidence for Tool Behavior." *Science*, May 6, 1988.
"New Hominid Fossils from the Swartkrans Formation (1979-1986 Excavations): Postcranial Specimens." *American Journal of Physical Anthropology*, March 5, 1989.
Takabayashi, Tokuharu. "The First Japanese-Congolese Mokele-Mbembe Expeditions." *Cryptozoology*, 1988, Vol. 7, p. 66.
Temple, Stanley A. "Plant-Animal Mutualism: Coevolution with Dodo Leads to Near Extinction of Plant." *Science*, August 26, 1977.
Thornton, Mary. "Seven Years Later, Jimmy Hoffa Case Is Still a Mystery." *Washington Post*, July 31, 1982.
Tomalin, Nicholas. "The Last, Tragic Voyage of Donald Crowhurst." *Sunday Times Weekly Review*, July 27, 1969.
Trevor-Roper, Hugh. "Martin Bormann Was Last Seen Definitely in a Tank in Berlin on May 2, 1945. Does He Live?" *New York Times*, January 14, 1973.
"Tuatara Tango." *Discover*, April 1989.
Vogel, Shawna. "Face to Face with a Living Fossil." *Discover*, March 1988.
Waldrop, M. Mitchell. "After the Fall." *Science*, February 26, 1988.
Walker, Alan, and Mark Teaford. "The Hunt for Proconsul." *Scientific American*, January 1989.
Warren, William. "Is Jim Thompson Alive and Well in Asia?" *New York Times Magazine*, April 21, 1968.
Weaver, Kenneth F. "The Search for Our Ancestors." *National Geographic*, November 1985.
Wilcove, David. "In Memory of Martha and Her Kind." *Audubon*, September 1989.
Woodbury, Richard. "The Skyjacker Who Vanished into Thin Air." *Life*, June 16, 1972.

Other Sources
Book Preservation Technologies. Washington, D.C.: Congress of the United States, 1988.
Maddow, Ben, and Terry Sanders. "Slow Fires: On the Preservation of the Human Record." Transcript of film. American Film Foundation. Washington, D.C.: Council on Library Resources, 1987.
Young, Christine. "Nitrate Films in the Public Institution." Technical Leaflet 169. *History News*, Vol. 44, no. 4. Nashville: American Association for State and Local History, July/August 1989.
Witten, A. J., and Wendell C. King. "Sensing Buried Waste." Manuscript by contractor of the U.S. Government under contract no. DE-AC05-840R21400. Washington, D.C.: U.S. Department of Energy, no date.

INDEX

Numerals in italics indicate an illustration of the subject mentioned.

Time-Life Books is a division of Time Life Inc.,
a wholly owned subsidiary of
THE TIME INC. BOOK COMPANY

TIME-LIFE BOOKS

Managing Editor: Thomas H. Flaherty
Director of Editorial Resources:
Elise D. Ritter-Clough
Director of Photography and Research:
John Conrad Weiser
Editorial Board: Dale M. Brown, Roberta Conlan,
Laura Foreman, Lee Hassig, Jim Hicks,
Blaine Marshall, Rita Thievon Mullin, Henry
Woodhead

PUBLISHER: Joseph J. Ward

Associate Publisher: Ann M. Mirabito
Editorial Director: Russell B. Adams, Jr.
Marketing Director: Anne C. Everhart
Director of Design: Louis Klein
Production Manager: Prudence G. Harris
Supervisor of Quality Control: James King

Editorial Operations
Production: Celia Beattie
Library: Louise D. Forstall
Computer Composition: Deborah G. Tait (Manager),
Monika D. Thayer, Janet Barnes Syring,
Lillian Daniels

Library of Congress
Cataloging in Publication Data
Vanishings / by the editors of Time-Life Books.
p.   cm.   (Library of curious and unusual facts).
Includes bibliographical references.
ISBN 0-8094-7687-8
ISBN 0-8094-7688-6 (lib. bdg.)
1. Curiosities and wonders.
I. Time-Life Books. II. Series.
AG243.V26 1990
031.02—dc20   90-35546 CIP

LIBRARY OF CURIOUS AND UNUSUAL FACTS

SERIES EDITOR: Russell B. Adams, Jr.
Series Administrator: Elise D. Ritter-Clough
Designer: Susan K. White
Associate Editor: Sally Collins (pictures)

Editorial Staff for *Vanishings*
Text Editor: Carl A. Posey
Researchers: Charlotte Fullerton (principal), Mau-
reen McHugh, Robert H. Wooldridge, Jr.
Assistant Designer: Alan Pitts
Copy Coordinators: Jarelle S. Stein (principal),
Donna Carey
Picture Coordinator: Jennifer A. Iker
Editorial Assistant: Terry Ann Paredes

Special Contributors: Carole Douglis, Bruce
Friedland, Deborah Kent, Peter Pocock, George Russell, Chuck Smith, Daniel Stashower, Roberta Yared
(text); Andra H. Armstrong, Susan E. Arritt, Cather-
ine M. Chase, Helga R. Kohl (research); Hazel
Blumberg-McKee (index)

Correspondents: Elisabeth Kraemer-Singh (Bonn),
Christine Hinze (London), Christina Lieberman (New
York), Maria Vincenza Aloisi (Paris), Ann Natanson
(Rome).
Valuable assistance was also provided by Mehmet Ali
Kislali (Ankara); Mirka Gondicas (Athens); Nihal
Tamraz (Cairo); Barbara Gevene Hertz (Copenhagen);
Judy Aspinall, Lesley Coleman (London); Trini Ban-
drés (Madrid); Elizabeth Brown, Katheryn White (New
York); Ann Wise (Rome); Mary Johnson (Stockholm);
Dick Berry, Mieko Ikeda (Tokyo).

The Consultants:
John B. Carlson is an astronomer at the University
of Maryland and director of the Center for Archae-
oastronomy. He is the editor of the *Journal of Ar-
chaeoastronomy* and coauthor of *The Face of Ancient America.*

William R. Corliss, the general consultant for the
series, is a physicist-turned-writer who has spent the
last twenty-five years compiling collections of
anomalies in the fields of geophysics, geology, archaeology, astronomy, biology, and psychology. He
has written about science and technology for NASA,
the National Science Foundation, and the Energy
Research and Development Administration (among
others). Mr. Corliss is also the author of more than
thirty books on scientific mysteries.

Brian M. Fagan is an archaeologist and a professor
of anthropology at the University of California at
Santa Barbara. His publications include *The Adventure of Archeology, Return to Babylon, Elusive
Treasure,* and *The Rape of the Nile.*

Charles R. Reynolds, a magic consultant for Broadway shows, films, and television, is coauthor of
three books: *100 Years of Magic Posters; Houdini:
His Legend and His Magic;* and *Blackstone Book of
Magic and Illusion.* He has lectured to international
audiences on the psychology of deception.

Marcello Truzzi, a professor of sociology at Eastern
Michigan University, is director of the Center for
Scientific Anomalies Research (CSAR) and editor of
its journal, *Zetetic Scholar.*

Other Publications:
THE NEW FACE OF WAR
HOW THINGS WORK
WINGS OF WAR
CREATIVE EVERYDAY COOKING
COLLECTOR'S LIBRARY OF THE UNKNOWN
CLASSICS OF WORLD WAR II
AMERICAN COUNTRY
VOYAGE THROUGH THE UNIVERSE
THE THIRD REICH
THE TIME-LIFE GARDENER'S GUIDE
MYSTERIES OF THE UNKNOWN
TIME FRAME
FIX IT YOURSELF
FITNESS, HEALTH & NUTRITION
SUCCESSFUL PARENTING
HEALTHY HOME COOKING
UNDERSTANDING COMPUTERS
LIBRARY OF NATIONS
THE ENCHANTED WORLD
THE KODAK LIBRARY OF CREATIVE PHOTOGRAPHY
GREAT MEALS IN MINUTES
THE CIVIL WAR
PLANET EARTH
COLLECTOR'S LIBRARY OF THE CIVIL WAR
THE EPIC OF FLIGHT
THE GOOD COOK
WORLD WAR II
HOME REPAIR AND IMPROVEMENT
THE OLD WEST

*For information on and a full description of any of
the Time-Life Books series listed above, please call
1-800-621-7026 or write:*
Reader Information
Time-Life Customer Service
P.O. Box C-32068
Richmond, Virginia 23261-2068

This volume is one in a series that explores
astounding but surprisingly true events in history,
science, nature, and human conduct. Other books in
the series include:

Feats and Wisdom of the Ancients
Mysteries of the Human Body
Forces of Nature
Amazing Animals
Inventive Genius
Lost Treasure